MITZVAH

By Alexandra

alexandraberro

Table of Contents

INTRO   Page 4

MITZI   Page 29

Hello, everyone, welcome to MITZVAH. This book is inspired by A BIPOLAR, A SCHIZOPHRENIC, AND A PODCAST. This is a super awesome podcast on Psych Central.com that is run by the indomitable Gabe Howard and Michelle Hammer. It is revolutionary because it is one of the few mental health podcasts out there that is made by individuals with mental illness for people with mental illness. I have heard that most mental health podcasts are made by family or by doctors, so having a podcast that is made by one of our number is truly a special thing.

Not only that, this podcast genuinely contains a lot of wisdom. I know I have learned a lot about life from listening to it. You can tell that Gabe Howard and Michelle Hammer have genuinely been through a lot. They've really been around, if you know what I mean. I've learned that it's impossible to change the past, among other things.

Now, this book is sort of like BSP and me's child. So there's a fair amount of "me" in these pages as well. Most of the stuff in this book has been addressed in the podcast as well (with the exception of a few topics, such as furries). However, I put my own unique spin on things. So I hope you will like it, although I know the tie in may not immediately be obvious.

Gabe, Michelle, I hope that MITZVAH does your podcast justice. You guys have done a great thing with A BIPOLAR, A SCHIZOPHRENIC, AND A PODCAST. I can never be as awesome and inspirational as you guys are, but I hope I at least come close. You know what they say...shoot for the stars, even if you miss, you land among the treetops. Which, frankly, sounds a lot more appetizing than landing among the stars.

Um...what else can I say? You and Michelle are my biggest mental health idols since Glenn (although i'm not in love with either of you...yet). So thank you, for all that you do. You guys truly are the Reality TV of mental health podcasts.

INTRO

So let me introduce myself. My name is Alexandra Berrocal, although online i'm known by other names. I am schizoaffective, a cat furry (or maybe therian), and non-binary when it comes to gender. Of these three labels, the schizoaffective label may be the most important one. Why? Because it was only when I figured out that one, got diagnosed, that the other two finally began to fall into place. When I realized I was schizoaffective, I finally understood how my mind and my emotions worked. I realized some of the traits of my emotions wasn't the fault of some rather upsetting things in my past. So it was easier for me to seperate my feelings of "flatness", if you will, with my "fursona" (which is pretty humanoid). And i've known for ages that i'm not really male or female (although i'm definitely more feminine than masculine). That really has nothing to do with my diagnosis. But it did become more clear to me, for reasons that I don't really understand. I have always been very conscious of the fact that i'm non binary when i've been on the dance floor (I generally go out dancing Thursday nights). I look at the men, and know I don't want to be a man. And I know i'm not a man. But then I look at the women, and I think they look beautiful. But I see how most of them are dressed, and I know I don't want to dress like them. My body doesn't particularly upset me, though. This confused me for a long time. I thought I should at least want to bind, to look more androgynous (I did for a while, want to look androgynous I mean). But now i'm ok with looking relatively female. And pronouns? I prefer feminine pronouns. I figured this out by being family to my nephew. I considered...well, what if I came out to my nephew? Would I want him to call me uncle? And for me, the answer would be no. I would rather be an aunt than an uncle, a mother than a father, and a queen than a king. So that tells you something right there. But yeah. I was confused by the fact that I didn't feel body dysphoria for a long time. I thought I should, if I was trans. And I was. And to a degree, I am. But...well...I don't feel body dysphoria. I suppose i'm lucky, although it would have been easier for me to figure myself out if I had been a typical transsexual instead of just non-binary. On the other hand, I hear body dysphoria is a horrible experience. So lucky me.

Anyone who doesn't live under a rock probably knows what a furry is. But most people don't know what therians are, so i'll explain. I've actually heard two different definitions of the therian/furry distinction. One definition is that therians actually believe they partially have the souls of animals in a human body. Furries simply like to dress up. It's kinda like the distinction between cross dressers and transgender people. The other definition is a bit more complex. The other definition says that fursonas are an integral part of who a furry is. Furries are more humanoid, therians are more animal like, and Otherkin are mythical. So yes. The definitions of furries vs therians change depending on who you talk to.

There is a process that many Otherkin people go through called Awakening. That's when people realize they are Otherkin. A lot of them think they are going crazy during this time. They aren't necessarily losing it. They're just entering a different state of being.

I have been through some version of Awakening...twice. Once was one time when Marty broke up with me. I thought he really was gone. I felt different. Not bad, not good. Just...very different from how I felt before. Recently, this happened again but much stronger. I experienced this over the course of a couple of days. That's one of the reasons I didn't go to Pride this year. The crowds would have been way too disconcerting for me. So Mother Superior (who didn't know about any of this) called me up, and we went to the zoo with her and her friend instead.

Mother Superior is a woman that I met last year at Passover dinner. She and I are on the same wavelength about many things, although she happens to be older than me by quite a few years. I call her Mother Superior because she is the closest thing I have to a Mother Superior. She and I both have felt a call to monastic life, but are not members of a faith that really provides this. Also, Mother Superior is an atheist. Unfortunately, there are no atheist convents as of 2019 or she would join up (and probably me as well). She covers her hair like I do, she is pretty modest, and we are both mostly celibate. It just feels like we're on the same wavelength, although we do not talk much. Oh, and she devotes her time to volunteer work (I wish I was that charitable). Well, ok, you should know she's not actually a Mother Superior. That's just the nickname I set for her on our Facebook chat page. Anyway...

I felt pretty lousy. Luckily, her friend turned out to be a good listener. I didn't tell her about the nonhuman stuff, just some of my personal problems. It still helped. They both stuffed me with food, too, always a plus.

I was actually really bored. But it was a safe space, I guess you could call it, for my Awakening. I didn't have any memories of past lives or anything like that. I just felt my feelings, which were, for the moment, non human. This went away after a couple of days.

There's only one reason that I truly believe I am a therian.

When I was around twelve, I became a huge fan of the WARRIORS book series by Erin Hunter. When I joined this fandom, I started to feel like I had pointy ears on the top of my head. I could retract them at will. I wasn't disturbed by this. I really liked them. But it caused problems because I assumed other people could see them when they couldn't. So one day, I decided to retract them permanently. And i've never been able to feel them again, no matter how hard I try. I sometimes wear cat ear jewelry now, as a sort of prosthetic.

Am I still a therian?

I haven't felt human since I was a freshman in high school. It feels a bit dumb to say this now, because right now I feel relatively normal. Right now I feel...ok. But sometimes when something really upsetting happens, like Marty leaving before his time or Jasper leaving...I feel genuinely strange. I can't really describe it. But it was Jasper leaving that was a big part of me realizing I was a furry because I just felt...so inhuman. And I don't mean inferior, either. I feel like humanity's equal, if not it's superior. But I do feel like I am outside of the species. Me having schizoaffective is a big part of this too. People with schizophrenia often have a flat affect (and blunted emotions too I think), and schizoaffective is a cross between bipolar and schizophrenia (as I understand it). So it's not surprising that my emotions would be different from the average person. Autism impacts this as well. I have autism.

Lest you think I am being sensitive, I want you to know that this really sucks. I would give almost anything to have normal human emotions. I am proud of the part of me that is a furry. I am proud to have autism (I don't really think autism is the cause of all this). But I would cure schizoaffective in a heartbeat if I could, for exactly this reason. It's a terrible thing to feel normal human emotions in your childhood and early adolescence, and to have them be suddenly wiped away. And it's not anyone's fault. I thought this happened to me because I was so traumatized by Halstrom that my emotions "ran away" if you will. It's a load off my shoulders to realize this just isn't so.

One example of my flatness was that Lynn was driving me home from support group once and missed my exit. We wound up going really far down the freeway. I thought, "Ok, she's going to take me to Las Vegas, traffick me, and sell me as a sex slave". I wasn't scared, though. I just was lying back, enjoying the ride, until Lynn finally turned around, got the exit right, and dropped me off at home.

One thing that bothers me about my illness is that i've pretty much lost my sense of wonder.
The last time I felt a sense of awe about anything was the time I was at Crater Lake with my mother. I'm not sure how old I was, although I know I was young. But that was the last time I felt awe over anything. I haven't felt it since, not even when looking up at a starry sky. Sad, huh?

But I can still appreciate beauty. I appreciate a beautiful person, a beautiful soul, or a beautiful landscape. I also love beautiful music. You could even say that I thirst for it. Beauty, that is. But yes. This is the reason I would take a pill to cure schizoaffective if I could. I would give anything to have my sense of wonder back. In a way, it's like I don't have a soul anymore. I tolerate that reality. I'm not ok with it. But I realize that I will probably never get it back, barring some really drastic thing happening to me. So I have to accept it and learn to live with it.

I don't believe that animals have souls either. I mean, I do believe that they have feelings. I believe they can feel deep love for humans and other animals. But I don't believe they can look at a starry sky and feel awe. That's a unique human thing. And that's why i'm not human. Or not human anymore at my core.

That said, I don't think it's ok to mistreat animals. Just because they don't have souls doesn't mean they don't suffer. I may have mentioned this in DEAD ON THE VERGE OF BLOOMING, but I believe we need to treat farm animals much, much better than we do. We also need to take care to treat dogs and cats well and to spay and neuter them. We have a huge problem with overpopulation. We also have a huge problem with overpopulation in humans, which is part of why I want to be fixed. I don't care if i'm not in a sexual relationship with a man. I want to be ready for anything, including rape.

But anyway.

I personally do not want kids because I am afraid I would molest them. This is not a rational fear. I have discussed the possibility with my psychologist many times, and she assures me that this fear is psychobabble. Lianna told me the same thing when I was seeing her. I also feel a lot like a child myself, and I personally feel that children should not be raising children. This is why I generally think that when a teenager gets pregnant, the fetus should be aborted. A teen still has a lot of growing up to do before they are ready to be parents. And I have a lot of growing up to do before I am ready to be a mother! Plus, I currently cannot care for a child. I am studying. I have no job. I cannot do both, because of the autism there is only so much I can handle in one day. I am not willing to give up my ambitions of becoming a psychologist to care for children. In terms of Mommy Wars, I am definitely a Career Woman. When my Mom went away to visit Dad (he is dying of cancer at the moment), it was all I could do to go to school, care for Nana, care for the cats, and care for the dog. I really had my hands full. I was greatly relieved when she returned, and resumed caring for the household.

Speaking of which, I really hate cleaning. I am profoundly grateful that my Mom does not make me do it often. This is another reason why I do not want to be a Desperate Housewife. If I marry, I would prefer to support the family financially and leave the cleaning and raising of kids to Mr. Right. I would love to have a house husband. Lianna says that gender expresses itself in relationships...I wonder what this says about me. Apparently this is common for women with autism, however. We do tend to be a bit more andro than your average lady.

That said, i'd rather give birth to a dog or cat than a human baby. I also wonder what this says about me.

Another aspect of having schizoaffective and autism is that I don't feel hurt so much as think hurt. I had a friend for a couple of months, dated him for a day, broke up, had a really explosive argument...it really ended badly for both of us. There were things he could have done better, but then again there were things I could have done better. I think he was probably right to block me. I think I am justified in being hurt. Him being freaked out and angry made me freaked out and angry. Not to mention hurt. And I ruminate on this endlessly. Frankly, I can't help it. Autism takes a random subject and cycles it through your head over and over. Sometimes this is beneficial. Not in this case.

BSP says that everyone makes mistakes, and that they should forgive themselves for them because they can't go back in time. So I need to acknowledge that I made mistakes, made amends as best I could, and in general did my best. Maybe my best wasn't very good, but it was still my best. So, as BSP puts it, I need to drink some tea with honey. Because I can't change the past.

That said, that friend has left a huge fucking hole in my heart. I didn't expect that at all. To me, he really was just a friend until I entered into a relationship with him. I have not shed a single tear, and yet I am in utter agony. I miss him deeply. Although he basically broke up with me because I did the memory/mental illness equivalent of falling down the stairs, and I resent that. He is also the Gordon Ramsay of exes.

Ouch.

So there are times when I watch porn. I am very visual, like a man. Words simply do not cut it for me. Neither does erotica. Oddly enough, pictures don't do it for me either. I need videos. And I know where to get them. PornHub has been great.

Usually, when a person is manic, they go out and fuck everything that moves. Some are bisexual. Some are straight. Some are gay. Some become bisexual when manic. Some are demi when manic. This can cause it's own share of issues. Basically, demisexuality is when you can only become sexually attracted to a person if you are emotionally close to them. No, this is not normal. If it was, casual sex would not be nearly as popular as it is. And I think I become a bit demi when manic.

Last time I was manic, I basically told my boyfriend at the time that I wanted his dick inside of me. Normally, a guy would be overjoyed to hear this. However, Marty is asexual, so this was not great news for our relationship. He is also trans. I did not know this at the time, but he does not actually have a dick. Luckily, I also mentioned his fingers as an alternative. He just blushed. So yeah. Actually, he told me later that that moment was the exact moment that he realized something was wrong with my mind. Because requesting sex from him was so out of character for me that I must be manic.

If you are requesting sex from a trans man (not Marty, different man), never tell a trans man that you are "done with dick", and you are interested in them because they don't have a dick. Plus, I should have thought things out a little more. I hate to say this, but I should have watched more porn. If I had, I might have realized I just wanted foreplay. But i'm still not exactly sure what i'd want out of that sort of relationship. I hope that's ok.

I realize I didn't talk hypersexuality and mental illness at all. But I guess I want you to know that since I am gray ace, I do not experience typical hypersexuaity...even when my mania is severe. I just look up a lot of porn. There. Done.

Once upon a time, I thought I was the Messiah. I thought it was up to me to save the world. I still think it's up to me to save the world. Me, Amnesty International, Greenpeace, the Unitarian Universalist Association, and various other people and organizations.

Honestly? Now, i'd just be happy to have a pulpit. I'd just be happy to give a couple of speeches about what being the Messiah of College Hospital Cerritos was like. But you know what's not fair?

So i'm manic. I'm getting a pizza at 7/11 with my Mom. I am texting my boyfriend, who is Orthodox Jewish. He is talking about how the Messiah will arrive when humanity has run out of time.

"But that's exactly what G-d told me!" I told him. "G-d told me that humanity has run out of time!"

I think he paused for a moment. And then he completely changed his tack.

"G-d will let us know when humanity has run out of time," he said.

Isn't that stupid? If literally the only definition of Messiah is the person who cries the alarm when humanity has run out of time, then I am the Messiah! And no pill can take that away from me! Or doctor! Or therapist! Or boyfriend, even!

So it really is up to me to sound the alarm. Nobody else realizes how urgent this situation is. It's like we're all moving through taffy, with less than ten seconds on the clock.

"I cannot tell them that this is the eleventh hour. I am sorry," he said.

"I will tell them to be kind to one another," he said.

Marty did not think particularly well of therians, furries, or Otherkin. He thought they needed therapy. Admittedly, all he knew of them was this one Youtube video that he saw of this man who came out. He started crapping in a cage. He insisted on buying really expensive fursuits that put the whole family in debt. I think he even insisted on going around on all fours in public. Anyone who saw that video would think we were all insane and needed therapy. Overall, this video did not present a particularly flattering portrait of our community. But I find it upsetting that Marty formed his opinion of us by watching one video. I mean, what the hell? Couldn't he at least have done his research before forming such a strong opinion? That's the best argument I can make. Because he's right, that guy really was out of control.

I didn't know that I was a furry yet, so Marty's low opinion and the video didn't really upset me. But looking back, that video was a modern day freak show. Some people will do anything to laugh at anyone who is perceived as being different from them. That's why freak shows used to be so popular. And YouTube seems to be slowly taking it's place. But I wish that video would have presented a more balanced view of our community, instead of painting us as freaks who need therapy.

Here's one remark from Marty that hurt: "Well, of course she left him. She, like most women, would be looking for something better in her marriage."

Something better? As if (barring abuse) one person was better than another! As if the man was somehow less than anyone else because he happened to have a fursona! Admittedly, the man needed to learn to be a bit more reasonable. But really? Something better in her marriage? I am appalled!

Passing for normal has never been an issue for me. I've always been able to pass for neurotypical. I am so calm that people would never know I was schizoaffective. I am in school, doing fairly well. I may live life on a slower pace than the average person, but at least I can live life. And autism? Easy to hide. One time, a church lady said she'd know I was autistic if she knew what to watch for. And Marty knew I was autistic right off the bat. But otherwise, people always told me they would never be able to tell I was autistic if I didn't tell them. As a result, I feel a certain disconnect from the autism community. So many of them, even so-called "high functioning" ones, seem to be much more symptomatic than I am. I feel like my diagnosis just does not fit. I mean, it does in some ways. Just in more subtle ways than the average autistic. But I don't really identify with the autism community at all. I feel sympathy, not empathy. I think the autism community can be a little ridiculous in some ways. Like, so-called "low-functioning" autistics are clearly impaired by having autism. You can't say that autism is this great thing in all cases. I agree that Applied Behavioral Analysis is bad (it focuses too much on behavior and compliance as measures of success). I agree that shock should never be used on Autistics. But that's about where the similarities end, off the top of my head.

I understand why some parents want a cure for autism. However, I think these parents are barking up the wrong tree. Autism is a genetic disorder. It is formed in the genes. Genes would have to be changed. You can't change genes with a pill. It may be possible to develop a test to abort autistics before they are born. But do we really want to do that? If the gene test specified levels of functioning, so that low-functioning autistics could be aborted but leave medium and high functioning autistics untouched...I might support it. Might. Because this would still bring up some thorny questions, which I do not have the answer for.

I hope this essay sparks a conversation, not ends it.

The thing is, I trusted almost no one. My older "siblings" were too busy being obsessed with Les Miserables to pay attention to me. My girlfriend was too busy trying to hump me to try to understand me. And hell, she only came into play in the latter days. The other kids at the Center were fun, and I loved them dearly, but I wasn't ready to tell them how bad I was really feeling. I felt closest to my friend Ryan, without a doubt, but I shut that off because I didn't feel ready for an intimate relationship yet. And get this guys (and this is really sad)...I don't mean sexually intimate. I mean emotionally intimate. I felt so close to him that it really, really scared me. Every time he looked at me, it was like I was naked. Ok, so it wasn't quite like that (he was gay). But we both admitted to having feelings for one another. I backed out, because I was chicken.

I don't feel that way towards him anymore, but I have not had a similar feeling towards anyone since.

I didn't trust my Mom either. She liked to complain a lot, about almost everything. Every time she did that, I wanted to punch her in the face. I thought to myself that she had no idea how good she had it, and that I was the one who really had something to cry about. Yet I never breathed a peep. I felt a lot of guilt. I played a lot of Suffering Olympics with myself, telling myself starving kids in Africa had it worse and most teens in other countries would give anything for an education like mine. I felt like such an ungrateful brat. "Why can't you just let it go?" Mom once asked me in frustration. Let go of everything I believe in? Yeah, fat chance. I remember seeing a movie when I was a little kid, on our way home from Tepotzlan at the time. In one scene, one of the characters doesn't want to get up in the morning. One of the characters says, "Get up!" The other lady says, "Why?" I think she starts sobbing too. And the sad thing is, I could completely relate. I could never relate to any of the kids at Halstrom or UCLA, because none of them were being repeatedly forced to violate their integrity as people.

After my diagnosis, I (almost) trusted Lilith (my girlfriend) with some personal information. Specifically, I almost told her about my fears of conservative Islam being the one true faith...and me going to hell because I thought I was gay. I also wanted to tell her my concerns that I may be a pedophile. I remember when her parents had taken us out on errands (they never did this), and they were stopping by the pharmacy. They had gone in to get medicine, and (I think) candy for us. Lilith and I were sitting in the backseat together, and I was trying to get up the courage to tell her. I was just opening my mouth when...you guessed it...her parents came back. And I just couldn't say anything in front of them. So it goes.

When I tried to move in with Renne, I wasn't manic. I was desperate. My life had become so shitty that I was willing to do almost anything to change it, including leaving my family forever for a trans woman that I barely knew. I figured it would help more than all the self help books I was buying. Or even the stupid, stupid, Work of Byron Katie.

So yeah. I always felt alone.

One of the reasons I (kind of) like mania is that during that time, I get my emotions back. I can feel some awe at a beautiful sunset. It's like something that is normally sort of off-kilter in my brain, is finally set to rights. Don't get me wrong. I don't like mania nearly as much as my fellow bipolar and schizoaffective people. A lot of mentally ill people enjoy their manias. I don't. For most people, it leads to increased productivity and a bunch of other good stuff. For me, it usually leads to some very terrifying places very fast. Before I thought I was the Messiah, I thought my boyfriend had set the Mossad on me. That's the Israeli CIA (Central Intelligence Agency), in case you didn't know. And they are very feared throughout the world. I wasn't mad at my boyfriend at all. But I was somewhat scared. But then I thought, "The Israeli CIA probably has better things to do than hack into the computer of a lone American BDS supporter." Just like that, the delusion was gone. In fact, I was able to think my way out of all of the delusional thinking I was going through at the time. I am very proud of this. The one delusion I wasn't able to reason myself out of was the delusion that I was the Messiah. That was the one that sunk me in the end, and took me to the hospital.

I actually started out not believing in G-d at all. I lost my faith. But I believed that it was my duty to pretend to be the Messiah, because I knew that someone claiming to be the Messiah would come along eventually and they would not be the real deal. So I knew I had to step up to the bat. It was only when I entered the hospital that I started believing in G-d, and started to believe that I truly was the Messiah. But I think you can tell that I define Messiah a bit differently from most mainstream religions. Then I had my conversion experience. So you could say that G-d played a trick on me. And spiritually, there is nothing I love more than trickster Gods. I was drawn to Coyote for a long time, and to a lesser degree Raven. I gave all that up when I went monotheistic, but that doesn't mean I don't appreciate a good trick. Or a good practical joke, in this case.

That said, I love depression too. I know this sounds really weird, but I love it. Because it's yet another excuse to feel. Most people don't like depression. But since i've been put on meds, i've never needed to be hospitalized for depression. My depression is nowhere near as bad as it used to be. I never have suicidal thoughts anymore. So for me, depression is much less dangerous than mania. I just feel really really sad, which is a-ok with me. Sadness is a natural part of life. I should be feeling sad once in a while. I would be really worried if I wasn't. Admittedly, depression is not fun. It is not fun at all. But it isn't this horrible thing that I dread and live in fear of. I don't live in fear of mania either, but I am always on the watch for it because it is a sneaky bastard. Depression isn't sneaky. You always know when you are depressed. So I don't have to constantly watch for depression.

I used to know a really badass woman named Vanessa. She had major depression. And she was able to accomplish so much. She has a travel blog. And she has really been around. A few years ago, she travelled to Egypt alone (around the time of the Arab Spring too, I think) and was perfectly fine. This is the sort of intrepid adventures she can get up to. I wish I could do that. But I can never travel outside my time zone alone, because I always need someone with me to watch for mania. So I can't be nearly as much of a badass as I otherwise would be. This is why I sometimes wish I had major depression instead of schizoaffective. On the other hand, many depressives wish they had bipolar or schizoaffective instead of depression because they wish they could get manic. Which I suppose I understand.

The grass is always greener on the other side.

It has been a real relief to me to realize that being sent to Halstrom at ninth grade was not the cause of my current...lack of emotion? I'm not sure. I definitely feel remorse. I'm not a psychopath. I definitely feel a lot of remorse for how I acted in the past towards certain people. I also felt a lot of remorse when I had a crush on young Hunter, because I thought a sixteen year old should not be in love with a thirteen year old. Whether I feel love is a harder question to answer. I always tell my Mom I love her. I wouldn't contest that. But it's not a very emotional sort of love. It's gratitude to her for caring for me all these years and continuing to care for me. It's loyalty. It's the fact that i'd do anything she tells me to, even if it's something I don't want. I always like her cooking, too! I also trust her to love me. I don't tell her everything that's going on with my life, because there is some information that I just don't trust her with. I've learned that I can't go to her with everything. That's what Kristen and Lynn are for. But I do go to her for certain things.

I shared her bed for a really long time. Kristen eventually told us to cut it out, because she thought it was causing issues in our relationship. So we've been in separate beds ever since. That is ok with me. At least I have the dog. But Kristen once said that I am in a relationship with my Mother. That may be true. It obviously isn't incestuous, but I think it may be closer than many adults my age. For one thing, i'm still a dependant. So I still depend on her for almost everything. Most people my age are more independent than I am, although I am fairly independent. After all, I don't depend on her for transportation and I largely live my own life. But still...still...

I don't know what i'm going to do when she dies. I am going to be absolutely devastated. I may even need to be hospitalized again. I don't know if I will be independent by then (I hope I will be). But even so, I will still be absolutely wrecked. Because my Mom has been the one constant person in my life. I may have hated her at times, but she was always there for me. She always kept a nice house, put food on the table, and stuff like that. When she started dating Dennis, I wasn't devastated because I felt like she was cheating on my father. I felt devastated because I felt like she was cheating on me. Call it incestuous if you will, but that's exactly how I felt.

I grew to like Dennis in time, although we always had a pretty contentious relationship. Mom says there was a time when we were close. I have no memory of that. I just remember all the fighting we used to do, especially when I entered Halstrom.
When Dennis and I fought, it was more than just child's play. However, neither of us were seriously out to injure the other. It's a really hard thing to explain unless you've been through it yourself. When I say fights, I of course mean physical fights. I often provoked him physically until he'd react by hitting me. I enjoyed this, so I kept provoking him. He often aimed for my elbow. He wanted to hit my funny bone so that i'd really learn a lesson. And one time he did, and it wasn't fun. However, I kept a straight face the entire time. I knew that if I let him know he had reached his goal, I was done for and he'd know where to aim from here on out.

Sometimes he'd say mean things to me when we were fighting. He'd say things like, "You need to learn to swim with the sharks. You aren't learning how to swim with the sharks." Or, basically, "You should be in public school, not homeschooled like you are." In all fairness, I didn't tell either of my parents about the Handbook for a very, very long time. And even when I told my Mom about it and asked her to read excerpts, she didn't really get it. She read the fiery anti-school tract and immediately suggested boarding school for me. This would have been nothing less than psychological torture. I would be at school constantly, they would have been running my life constantly, and I would have had no escape. I probably would have preferred jail, because at least there you are not expected to be happy. It is taken for granted that your life is being run for you, and that you have no freedom at all. Same as boarding school.

So yeah, both of my parents were sort of clueless as to what was really going on with me.

My psychologist, Kristen, thinks that I do have emotions. She says that since they are not very strong, however, they do not really "ping" on my emotional radar. So I basically have emotions but don't really know it. She's known me all my life. Also, this explanation does "feel" right. Because I do feel some emotion. I'm not completely flat, although I am pretty flat.

Kristen also thinks my flatness is caused by the autism. I strongly disagree. I had strong emotions as a child. That went out the window freshman year of high school. I have been autistic all my life. I did not "become" autistic in my freshman year. If my flatness was caused by autism, it would be a lifelong thing. But it hasn't been. I know it hasn't been.

I think the likely explanation is the "schizo" in schizoaffective. This was the main reason why I pushed for a re-diagnosis. Schizophrenics commonly have a flat affect. I know this from observing Dennis, who is also schizoaffective. They tend not to be very emotional people. Now, I don't have a flat affect at all. I emote in a very emotional way. I pass for normal, in other words. Schizophrenia tends to strike in young adulthood, but can happen earlier. If I truly am schizoaffective, this symptom may have struck me first, when I had no idea what it was, and chalked it up to extreme trauma or being Otherkin. See? This is why labels matter!

I definitely have moods. My psychologist has observed me being very up, very down, and everything in between. But feelings? I'm not so sure. When I "feel" something, it tends to act out as a story in my brain. This can make it very difficult to figure out what i'm actually feeling, or if it may be a mix of feelings. Mom says I should write these stories down, but I prefer nonfiction to fiction. I'm also afraid i'd sit down at the laptop and suddenly develop writers block. That doesn't really happen to me with nonfiction. Once i've made my mind up to write something, nothing can stop me. But I have all these bizarre stories in my head, and i'm afraid people would think I was weird if I shared them. They tend to involve Isaiah a lot these days, who is someone that I really miss despite the fact that he threatened to stalk me last time I saw him. So despite the fact that I only have moods these days...people can still hurt my feelings and people can hurt them very badly.

I am going to lift a story from the podcast to make a point.

Before Gabe was diagnosed with bipolar disorder (and i'm assuming anxiety as well), he weighed somewhere around 550 pounds. When he got anxiety attacks, he mistook them for physical hunger. So when he'd get an anxiety attack (which was pretty frequently back then), he would eat a ridiculous amount of food. I mean, he ate a ridiculous amount of food in general...but I think (Gabe confirm this) he started eating gargantuan amounts of food in response to his anxiety, and mistaking anxiety for hunger.

Now do you see why labels are important?

If you still don't, let me explain. If Gabe had known that what he was going through was an anxiety attack and not physical hunger, he would not have gained all of that weight. Instead, he would have been on an antianxiety medication, and would have been able to pop a pill whenever he was feeling poorly. He would have been able to avoid all the pain and trouble that came with being overweight, such as that surgery thing that they do on a lot of obese people these days.

Labels increase self awareness. There is a reason that there is a "naming the demons" meditation in Buddhism. Naming things gives us a certain power over them. It allows us not to be affected by them so much. People also tend to think new words are superfluous. They're not. People using new words really are different, and they need terms to describe that. It's not enough to say i'm a woman with a man. A nonbinary person is not the same as a woman. I know the difference can be hard to pick up, but it's there for the person who has felt different all of their life. And it shouldn't just be chalked up to being a special snowflake. You see, people who fight neologisms at heart tend to think people are all the same and that they're creating new words for fun. They're not. They are having a different experience from the rest of the world, and need a way to describe what they are going through. And no, it's not always fun. For some, it is even a drag.

No pun intended.

Most of the time, in most contexts, I prefer to be treated like an ordinary human being. I don't need people to call me "Kitty". I don't usually purr or meow. I don't need to poop or pee in a litter box. I can use the toilet, thanks. I can talk, in ordinary verbal language (as long as it's English). I just want people to understand that in some ways, I am a cat at heart. I'm not a big cat person. I don't feel a need to be around cats much. I don't hate them, i'm just indifferent. If I met more people like me, that would be nice, but i'm not exactly starving for role models. Other therian/furry friends would be nice, though. But I obviously wouldn't pick friends just because they are like me. All I really ask for is understanding. I know that doesn't sound like much, but in some ways that's the hardest thing of all.

I feel much the same way about being non-binary. I don't really feel a need to use they/them pronouns. I don't want male pronouns either, i'm not a man. I'm 100% OK with female pronouns. I am an Aunt. If I gave birth or adopted a child, i'd be a mother. If I fucked my mother, i'd be a motherfucker. And so on. You get the idea.

I am more conscious of my gender on the dance floor than anywhere else. I am happy being a follow, mainly because I don't have to think. I don't want to learn how to be a lead. I don't really care about dancing with girls. I am happy dancing with guys most of the time. But I notice the women, and how they dress, and I know in my heart that I could never dress like that. I could never manage the hair and the makeup either. I've only seen one chick there who's look i'd like to emulate, and she was wearing a t-shirt and jeans. I generally wear a t-shirt and pants to the dance floor anyway. West Coast Swing is all about legs, so it's better not to hide them under a long skirt (unlike contra dancing, or square dancing where it doesn't matter either way). I never wear makeup. I wear a head wrap. I suppose I pass for female there, especially when I don't generally bind. Having a fairly curvy figure helps too. So I guess I look fairly feminine. Just less so than the other women there. Or maybe I look just as feminine, but in a different way. I genuinely don't know. I'll have to ask some guy there.

I'd be genuinely ok with whatever answer I get. I'm not insulted when people call me a man. Mom has called me her son twice, and although it's slightly confusing it's ok with me. Lamont once called me a man to insult me, and I just laughed inwardly. Dennis once said an old photo of me looked like a shemale, and I was actually quite flattered.

And please don't give me this "don't worry about labels" crap. I already explained why I hate that line of thinking. I'm not worrying about labels. If i'm worrying about anything, i'm worrying about identity.

So please respect that.

In many ways, i'm still trying to figure out who I am. Now that i'm out of that three-ringed-shitshow called high school, and i've found a decent course of study, and i'm studying, I find i'm not the person I used to be. I can be really caustic. I don't love animals as much as I used to. I have no desire to sing solos, unless maybe I start going to Temple again. All the stuff I was as a child, I no longer am. I'm not gay. I'm gray. Pride is not as important to me as it used to be. LGBTQ stuff is not as important to me as it used to be. I am still a writer, but that came along fairly late in the game. It's just that the things I like to do now are not the things I liked to do then. These days, you can't tear me away from any kind of screen. I used to love reading books. I pretty much no longer do. I used to want to garden. Now I consider that major drudgery. I still love music, but I listen instead of sing. I'd love to try rapping, but I don't know how to make that happen for me. It's like that Fugazi quote, "You can't be what you were, so you better just start by being who you are."

But who the hell am I? I definitely have a dark side. I can be toxic. I can be clueless. I wish this wasn't so. Believe me, I do.

I hurt enough already, thank you.

MITZI

Now that I have properly introduced myself, this story can really begin.

In an early episode of BSP (A BIPOLAR, A SCHIZOPHRENIC, AND A PODCAST), in a game of Two Truths and a Lie, Michelle reveals that once a guy wanted to bang her because "he always wanted to bang a Jewish chick". To be fair, I have never been on the receiving end of this sort of behavior. But it looks like I have dished it out, and completely by accident at that. And that is my regret.

I'm not going to say i'll change, because I don't want to disappoint anyone if I fail. Abusers always say they'll change, and when the victim lets them back into their life, they abuse them all over again. I don't want that to happen. You know what they say, as I would not be slave, so I would not be master.

I remember the time I cuddled with Marty when he didn't really want to. Absolutely inexcusable on my part. I should have noticed that he didn't want to cuddle. And it kills me that I didn't. He didn't say no outright. If he had said a clear no, I would not have cuddled with him. Which is still no excuse for what I did. I don't think about it a lot, but I have a hard time forgiving myself for that too. I wonder if I really deserve to forgive myself at all.

But yeah. I think most people consider me unfuckable, which is why i've never heard "I've always wanted to bang a crazy chick." Of course, who would say, "I've always wanted to bang a Unitarian Universalist!" There's also the fact that I seldom interact with people I don't know, which makes dating difficult in most cases. And I think we can all acknowledge that internet dating is very different from real life dating. On the internet, people see a very different version of you than normal. But I find this topic sort of tiring.

However, I will say that I view overcuddling (that's what I call this) through the lens of sexual harassment. I don't really know why this is. I just do. And I completely understand Marty's point of view on this issue, because my Dad overcuddled me when I visited him on vacation when I was little. I never really got over it. It may still affect our relationship (or largely lack thereof) today. So I can understand how something like that would affect a person. And if Marty never talks to me again, or never wants to see me again because of that incident, I completely understand.

    I think he probably broke up with me more because he felt we had nothing in common, but still.

I'm going to switch the topic to guns, since Gabe and Michelle did a podcast on guns once. I think.

I would never own a gun. Not only do I think it is wrong to do so, but I don't rely on it for hunting or fishing (both noble hobbies by the way). I'm also afraid of what I would do with it in the throes of depression or mania. Last time I was manic, I was considering conducting a mass shooting. It was just a casual thought, but it's enough to really scare me. And depression...well, that's obvious. I could easily use a gun to commit suicide. Bipolar, schizoaffective, and depressed people deal with the existence of guns in a variety of ways. Some have family care for their guns for them. Others go to the range and go home.

But I would like to talk about other weapons as well. Like spears, swords, tridents, things like that. When I was little, I always wanted to take Edged Weapons at my local dojo. Nowadays, I still want to...but think it would be a dumb idea for me. Ditto for swords, even though I really love them. A sword is not a gun, sure. But what if I got really manic during practice? I could really hurt the people around me by being reckless. And reckless is a quality you do not want with a sword in hand.

Recklessness is a quality you do not want in general, and that is why mania can be so debilitating. Mania causes us to make all kinds of reckless decisions. For someone with a reckless personality, it can be hard to tell where mania ends and personality begins. I'm not reckless. It's just a thought.

I don't take the Christian concept of sin very seriously because i'm not Christian. However, I do take the Jewish concept of sin seriously. I'm not Jewish, but their concept of sin is a useful concept for me to have in my spiritual toolbox. Basically, in Judaism, their concept of sin is that sin is what happens when you "miss the mark". It is what happens when you are aiming for something higher, and miss the proverbial target instead. I relate to this very deeply, because the worst things I have ever done in my life happened when I was trying to help someone or otherwise trying to do a good deed (or a mitzvah) in Judaism.

Take Jude. I basically annoyed the shit out of him, made his anxiety worse, made fun of his identity, and made light of his identity at times in the name of trying to help him with his depression. I was only a child, but that was still pretty bad, and I was still responsible for my actions.

When I coerce-cuddled Marty, I was simply trying to show affection. I had no idea that I was in reality doing something much more sinister.

When I broke my Dad's heart, I didn't mean to injure him. I simply needed some privacy, and I was afraid.

When I left my Aunt, I didn't mean to make her life worse. I was simply growing up. I don't mean that we outgrow kin. But older kids and teens do not typically hang out with their uncles and aunts for extended periods of time. Luckily, she eventually gave me grace because she saw I had a mental illness when no one else did.

I didn't mean to turn my back on my Hispanic heritage. I was simply pursuing life in America.

These are all of the ways I have missed the mark.

On that topic, let's talk about person-first language. You may wonder how this relates to the above. Well, some people think that identity-first language reduces a person to one identity, and crowds out other aspects of their life. The trouble with that is that with Autism, the person and the "disability" cannot be separated so easily. Autism affects the way personality develops. That's not to say all Autistics are the same. However, many of us share certain common threads. So the notion that we are somehow separate from our disability is ridiculous. And that is why I am Autistic, and not a "person living with Autism".

Schizoaffective is a little more complex. I have not been schizoaffective all my life. My illness began at 17 officially, although it really began in 5th grade when I began having anxiety about being raped. Before then, though, I was just a normal child with the occasional sleep problem. However, the genetics for schizoaffective were probably always there. Theoretically, though, you could separate the person from the disability...provided they have none of the negative symptoms of schizophrenia such as a flat affect. The negative symptoms of schizophrenia and autism are so similar, though, as I understand it, that they are a mutually exclusive diagnosis. It's also hard to tell where schizoaffective ends and autism begins. So that just snarls things up further.

Complicated, huh?

It's better to ask a disabled person whether they prefer person-first language or identity-first language. Their answers may vary, or surprise you. I know person-first is very popular these days, because of the above. But I prefer identity-first language, as do many Autistics on the internet. I don't think that Autism or Schizoaffective is such a horrible thing that I need to "separate" myself from it or prove that I am "more than that". I think such thinking actually contributes to stigma. I don't need to "rise above" my illness. It is a part of me.

If I didn't have any mental illness (I don't count Autism as a mental illness), I would basically go on a permanent backpacking/kayaking/sailing trip. And I would take my nephew with me, if he was single and also didn't have any family to stay with. I have known my nephew for approximately one and a half years, and we have only had two arguments. The first one ended in him apologizing to me for his behavior. The second one ended in me sort of semi apologizing to him, and then the debate no longer mattering because he switched alters and finally got some sleep.

Oh yeah. I should tell you, Nathan is a multiple personality system. There are around 20 alters in the system, and I love all the ones that i've met. Sometimes I feel like i'm meeting new people over and over, but it doesn't bother me. I would never tell him this to his face, but I love him. And I know love is a scary word for him. So I try to show it in other ways, like talking to him semi-regularly and trying to be there for him when he needs me. I love you is a pretty shallow statement anyway.

I wish he lived with me, but I don't have the resources to care for a teen. Plus, he's a pretty patriotic Canadian...so I don't think he would abandon his country. Luckily, he lives with a loving adoptive family that supports him being transgender. They also support him having DID and they don't think he's lying. Which is good.

I don't think he's lying either, but I also don't really care if he's lying or not. I just care about being there for him whenever he needs me. I care about him being safe. I care about him being well. And i'm happy that by and large, he has those things.

Maybe someday we will travel together.

I used to binge eat a lot. I wasn't as bad as some other people you may have heard of. I wasn't nearly as bad as Gabe was. I didn't eat entire sheet cakes. I didn't devour multiple pizzas at a time. However, it was bad enough that, at the time, I was quite overweight. And I haven't lost any weight since then. I've gained it. I'm about 5'8", and I weigh about 205 ibs. I don't look it at all. I'm very well-proportioned. When I tell people, they are always astonished. My old friend Tea even once said that it must be muscle, and that I don't look fat at all.

However, my Mom was extremely worried about it. She was concerned enough that she made me work out every day (I was homeschooled, but didn't mind this), and put me on a diet (I minded this very much.) It didn't really help. All it did was make both of us upset. My extra weight didn't really bother me. However, my inability to lose weight really bothered my Mom. She used to be pretty crazy about it too. After my diagnosis, I once ate a cookie at support group. Mom got wind, took me aside, and aimed some angry and choice words my way. Joel (he still attended at the time), thought she needed an atypical antipsychotic. Those were his words too. Mom compared me eating the cookie to me using alcohol or drugs.

Jenny Craig did not help me have a more balanced relationship with food. If anything, it made it worse. What is the first thing you think of when someone tells you, "Don't think of a pink elephant?" A pink fucking elephant, of course. Now, things were different for Gabe. I acknowledge that. But for me, Jenny Craig completely disrupted my life for no reason and did more harm than good. I would probably tell my past Mom, knowing what I do today, to just keep my past self as busy as possible so she won't be preoccupied with food, overeat, and gain weight. But I was also having a lot of emotional issues that frankly, were just not being addressed. School being the top. So dieting was doomed to fail from the start.

I am lucky. I will admit that I am lucky. And I genuinely mean it. I am blessed.

However, it seems like this has become a common trope in disabled circles...for people with physical disabilities as well as mental illness. We are all expected to count our blessings, even when life sucks. And it does suck sometimes. And every time we complain, people say, "Oh, but you're so lucky!" And it gets annoying at best. This is one where I have been on the giving end more on the receiving end. It was a certain Alyxander who showed me that using this trope on a disabled person is ableist. I am not sure exactly why. But it is something I try to remember. And it is something you should remember too.

I have a loving family, a nice home, and good medical care. I did not always have those things. My family used to mean well, but make my life extremely difficult. I always had a nice home, but somehow that doesn't feel so important when you're truly miserable. Plus, I had untreated mental illness. So I wouldn't call that good medical care. But I also wouldn't say that's anyone's fault. Even though those years were absolutely terrible, my family just didn't know any better and that's why I forgive them.

And yes, those years were terrible. I had three of the best friends you could ask for, who were the best part of those years. I had children in my life who adored me, whom I adored. In the latter days, I had the LGBT Center, which was my saving grace. But I was still sad. I hid it well, but I had persistent feelings of sadness and shame almost all of the time.

So fuck anyone who says I was lucky. I am lucky now. I was not lucky then.

In one episode of A BIPOLAR, A SCHIZOPHRENIC, AND A PODCAST, Michelle laments the unfortunate name of a certain class of medications. These medications are called anti-psychotics. She complains that when you tell someone you take an anti-psychotic (which I do as well, by the way), people go, "Oooooh! Psychotic? You're psycho?" Or something like that. Now, I have never gotten that reaction. But on the other hand, I don't run around telling people that I take anti-psychotic medications. My old Intro to Psych professor also laments the unfortunate ramifications of the word "psychotic", and the tendency for people to associate psychotic with dangerous and out of control.

By the way, I don't appreciate those stupid t-shirts that say, "I put the HOT in psycHOTic". Psychotic people should never be thought of as sexy. I would go so far as to say that those sorts of slogans encourage sexual assault of the mentally ill, as if our lives weren't hard enough already. Besides, who the hell would want to fetishize mental illness? Is there some silent subculture out there that I don't know about? Someone who gets off at the sight of my pills? Someone who would consider a psych ward hot dating space?

Oh no. Now I know how trans people must feel...

Speaking of sexual assault of the mentally ill, I have a story for you all. I already told it in DEAD, and I generally try not to repeat myself, but people need to know that sometimes these things happen on psych wards.

Me and Victoria were sitting in our room minding our own beeswax. Suddenly, about four nurses come in. One of them says, "Victoria, we are going to put Geodone and Ativan up your butt."

I think they actually said shove.

Something about the whole situation felt really wrong. So I said, "I can't watch this," and stood in the doorway with my back to Victoria. There was silence. After a few minutes, the nurses started to leave the room.

"What the hell?" I asked one of the nurses.

"Alexandra, we only give meds orally here," the nurse said.

A few days later…

"Victoria," I asked her, "Was I hallucinating about the pills?"

"No," Victoria replied.

So I went to Dayroom. I went to the Head Nurse. "Hey, what do you guys do here in cases of sexual assault?"

The head nurse said, "We tell them to file a complaint."

"Got it," I said.

"Look, when these things happen…there is supposed to be at least one woman present. There was a woman, wasn't there?"

I didn't answer her. But I told Victoria to file a complaint. And bless her, she began bringing me cups of water.

When I told my psychologist this story, she said that sometimes psych ward staff will put pills up a patient's butt as a last resort. She said it is just another way to get meds into a patient's system. I call bullshit. If this were real, IVs would be put up people's butts all the time. Food would be put up the butt of hunger-striking prisoners all the time, and it wouldn't be seen as a form of torture like it currently is.

Another upsetting thing about psych wards is that they generally do not take concerns about safety seriously. There was this one woman on the Ward named Jill who had a tendency to yell at people. She, looking back, was clearly very delusional herself although she could be insightful about some things. She was friends with a guy named Paul, who was also friends with me. She was ok with me when I first arrived, but gradually became worse and worse and in general devolved as a person. She became this horribly angry, anti-Semitic person who thought I was white and that white women always get their way in life (pal, nobody does). I do worry sometimes that it was somehow my fault, but I was very sick myself. It's a wonder that I was able to help as many people as I did, even though I didn't talk to everyone on the Ward. I guess it's inevitable that I would make a few slip-ups on the way, like accidentally implying through my words that I was a Trump supporter (I hate him), when I was just trying to understand why Johanna would vote for him. I also wish I had spoken up when Johanna gleefully declared that there was no racism anymore (there is, big time). (You can tell i'm a liberal from here). Oh yeah, and I declared that my entire family were a bunch of welfare queens because we actually manage to make an OK living off of Social Security, which is a miracle on my family's part.

So I can see why Jill would be pissed off at me.

Johanna was far braver than I was. She was content to room with Jill, without asking for a room change. I did get a room change, but the people who were dumb enough to build this hospital built it with shared bathrooms, so it would be easy to get from one room to another without having to use the front door. The nurses would have no idea what you were doing. So I still didn't feel safe.

I kept requesting a unit change. Finally, during visiting hours, Jill walked by, flashed me, lunged at my visitor, and they finally gave me a fucking unit change. My next roomie was a fellow Wrapunzel Lady (what are the chances?) and she and a Holocaust Denier (ironic, I know) became my two new best friends. I miss them both to this day.

I understand missing Connie (the Wrapunzel Lady). She was pretty darned cool. Missing Isaiah (the Holocaust Denier) makes less sense. I affirm the Holocaust. I believe it happened. I am not interested in hearing about or learning about any other point of view on this subject. But he took me seriously when I said I was the Messiah. He offered to help me.

You guys all remember the whole Garden of Eden story, right? G-d creates the world, creates animals, creates people, puts them in Eden, tells them not to eat the apple, people eat the apple, they are cast out. Well, boy, do I have news for you about what happened to that apple.

The apple from the Garden of Eden is taking over. Think about it. The company pioneering most of the new technology in communications is called APPLE. The logo is of an apple with a bite taken out of it, representing the bite Adam and Eve took when they ate of the fruit and gained knowledge of good and evil. I would say this apple is doing very well for itself. It may very well be the most successful apple in history.

We are risking losing our Eden if we continue on the path we are on. I am not completely blaming technology, although it doesn't exactly help. We can use technology to save Eden. We can use technology to connect with one another in more meaningful ways (perhaps the most exciting thing about it). But we need to understand what we risk losing if we are not extremely careful. There is nothing quite like sitting outside and just talking to a flesh-and -blood human. And new technology may have more ramifications that I have not thought of yet.

This apple is leading us into a brand new world. And we should march forward with courage. As long as we do not lose our old world. And as long as we do not lose nature.

The concept of laughing at someone's mental illness and then claiming it is some bizarre form of empathy...is a strange practice that is observed in some mental health circles. I personally do not understand it at all. Not only do I not understand it, I find it highly insulting. When people laugh at me when I am talking about my past delusions, I take it as a very hard slight...even when the "laughers" have mental illness themselves. Now, i've been around the block. I've believed I was the Messiah (which is very common actually). I've believed a giant spider is trying to rape me. Neither is funny to experience. Mental illness in general is not funny.

Would we do this to people with cancer? Cancer is life threatening, just like I believe mental illness is. If someone vomited in a chemo support group, or (here's a better metaphor), talked about losing her hair...would we laugh? Of course not. We recognize cancer as a serious thing. We even recognize hair loss as a fairly serious thing, because there are all kinds of services out there to help cancer patients feel beautiful through chemo. I'm proud to say that the Wrapunzel Foundation is one of them. I think.

The point is, it does not serve our cause to treat mental illness like a joke. It is also extremely hurtful to someone who has just gotten out of the hospital, and might not have kicked all of their delusions yet. This might feel really personal to them. It certainly felt personal to me, when I was laughed at. Mental illness is a life-threatening illness when untreated, either by suicide or by forcing the person to ruin their life. There is nothing remotely funny about that. So I don't understand why people think it is ok to laugh.

Now, Joel understands that I do not like this sort of behavior so he avoids doing it to me. But he has also said something along the lines of, "She just doesn't understand about laughing in sympathy yet." And G-d, I hope that day never arrives.

I've been accused of basically faking all of my disabilities by someone who was supposed to be my friend. I remember him saying, "Autism...bipolar...all the trendy diagnoses."

Do you know why this is rude?

I lost the woman I loved because of bipolar disorder. If I hadn't developed what we thought at the time was bipolar, I would have moved up to Northern California to be with Renne. Maybe our relationship would have gone well, maybe it wouldn't have. Maybe I would have been able to sustain myself up there, maybe not. But if I hadn't developed mental illness, there is a chance that she wouldn't have been at that fateful intersection, in the wrong time and place. Maybe she would have been hanging out with me, in another location. Either way, there is a small chance that she would still be alive today. But she's not. She was hit by a car and died. And I still have a heartbeat, schizoaffective and living in Southern California. Fuck, sometimes life is just not fair.

And autism? I was diagnosed when I was practically a toddler, way too young to be wondering what was "trendy". I had special ed. I had special therapy. I had almost no friends growing up. I developed a bizarre sense of humor from having online friends. When I was in sixth grade, I was put in a school for the disabled. At seventh, I was put in a school specifically for autistic children. A lot of time and money put in for something that was just a trend, that I didn't even get to decide for myself. I think you know what I would have chosen by now.

So yeah. Neil can go fuck himself. And no, I do not want to watch. And I do not need "Orgasmic Meditation" or whatever the hell it's called, to help me be less asexual. I mean, i'm technically graysexual. But I used to call myself asexual because that was the pole I gravitated most strongly towards. Now I realize that can confuse people in the extremely rare situation that I find myself wanting more. So now I identify as graysexual. It was the technically correct term to begin with anyway.

However, note that asexuals can still enjoy making out and foreplay and still be accepted as asexuals in the community. They can even desire sex in general, as long as it's not aimed at a specific person. Yeah, that part confuses me too.

Sorry for this little educational tidbit. I'll move on now. And Neil, no, you are not welcome to say i'm confused just because you are.

One of the people in my life who was most afraid of the stigma of mental illness was my former teacher, Priya. She said to my Mom once, something along the lines of, "You're so open about it! You need to be careful!" My step-Grandpa Pete was also concerned. I used to frequently wear a shirt that said, "Bipolar" on it. Pete worried that I was drawing stigma to myself by wearing it. I tried to wear the shirt at work once too, and had no issues. However, once I was wearing it and had to go to the main corporate offices for some reason. My boss saw the shirt, said, "That's risque" (word for word), and immediately gave me another shirt to change into. I changed back when I got home.

Why, people? Why? I was extremely open about my illness in the LGBTQ community, and got literally nothing but love and acceptance from them (except for one Pride event, where a passing lady said, "I wouldn't advertise that if I were you.") What on earth is holding the straights back? Are we still living in the age of mental institutions?

Admittedly, Pete grew up in a different time. This sort of thing was very hush-hush in olden days. But this isn't olden days. This is the 21st Century. We are supposed to be more enlightened now. We are supposed to be more open now. We are getting better about LGBTQ acceptance. What about the mentally ill? We are still portrayed poorly in media, that's for sure. People still say "That's so bipolar", "I'm so OCD" just like we used to say "That's so gay" and "That's so retarded".

Aren't you glad those fell out of fashion?

Seriously though, I once almost got kicked out of my home because I had written and published DEAD ON THE VERGE OF BLOOMING. Mom was so furious and hurt about what i'd written that she told me to get the hell out, basically. She thought that what i'd written was passing judgment on her. So I went upstairs to pack my things.

When I was on the stairs, wondering what I should pack (I already determined that I would go to my Grandma's or to Joel and Lynn's), my Mom said, "You can't just go."

I turned around.

And then began one of the most emotional exchanges of my entire life.

I don't remember what was said word for word. But I did say that if I had the chance to pick another mother, I wouldn't have. I would always have picked her. I meant it. And I do mean it. I told her I loved her. That's about all I remember. We were both crying. She said she was sorry for everything i'd gone through. But she said it in this really bitter, angry way. I still hadn't expected to ever get an apology for this stuff, even if it was an angry one. So that's why I cried...from a place in me that was really deep, that I hadn't even known was there.

We both needed some space after that. I took a short walk. I don't remember what she did. But I stayed home that day. I didn't get kicked out. And I still have a home to this day.

Mom still hasn't read all of DEAD. She's read all of the first part, about me and Renne. She hasn't read the parts about Marty, or about all the other people I have loved. She helped edit HEYA = HEYA (who says parents can't be good editors?). She hasn't read GARNETS or KOBIETA (they're not my best work), but she did help edit GALATEA. So you could say she's kind of in and out of my literary life.

Although I wish she'd finish DEAD, i'm ok with that.

Would I take a pill to cure autism?

Would I take a pill to cure schizoaffective?

Would I take a pill to cure school phobia?

All of these questions have different answers. That is to say, I would answer all of these questions differently. Surprised? You shouldn't be. For people with multiple mental illnesses...not all mental illnesses are equally debilitating. Some are more so, some are less so.

I would not take a magical pill to cure autism. My autism isn't debilitating enough to me that I feel the need for it to be "cured". Plus, I just don't think I would feel like myself without my autism. Having autism has influenced my life so profoundly that I just can't imagine life without it. Some things might be easier, sure, like having friends. However, I don't think the trade off is worth it.

However, I would take a magical pill to cure schizoaffective disorder. I have lived without it. I can imagine life without it. Schizoaffective significantly impairs my life. I have to watch myself all the time. I have to go to a special doctor. I have to go to a support group. I have to take special medicine. And despite these things, I still have slips sometimes. It's frustrating. There are things I wish I could do, that I can't because of schizoaffective, like travel alone. So you see how it is?

I would not take a magical pill to cure school phobia. Why? Well, for one thing, I grew out of it. But another thing is that the vast, vast, majority of the suffering caused by my school phobia was caused by the fact that my family and my psychologist were basically forcing me to stay in school and be triggered on a daily basis...and then come home and be triggered some more by my homework. If my parents had allowed me to drop out and attend community college, I would not have been triggered and thus would not have been impaired by school phobia. If my parents had allowed me to live the way I wanted to live, I also would not have been impaired by school phobia. So it wasn't school phobia that was the problem. It was my family and my psychologist. Thus, no need for a pill. I am also concerned about how such a pill would work. Would it wipe my memory? Would it make me so complacent that I no longer cared about my morality? Would it make me so manic that I would no longer care?

See, these are the kinds of questions you have to ask yourself.

By the way, I don't blame anyone who can't get decent healthcare in America today. You know where I wanted to go during my second episode? UCLA. I wanted to go to friggin UCLA, because I knew that I would get the best possible care there. But no. No, I went to College Hospital Cerritos. It goes to show that even G-d can't make it to UCLA these days.

We have such a broken healthcare system. Cerritos isn't the worst mental hospital out there. By my standards, I would rank it as "Ok". Half the time, it's the illness that is making the whole experience bad. And Cerritos needed me. Hell, they really needed a Messiah. So in a way, i'm glad I went. The other patients really needed inspiring, and I think I delivered on that even though I was a real asshole half the time.

Well, i'll just say this.

G-d has spoken.

Today is the Fourth of July, and today there was a 6.6 earthquake in Southern California. G-d is not pleased.

We as a society are becoming more and more preoccupied with sex and sexual things, while completely forgetting about the least of these (poor, refugees, homeless, etc.)

This is why we are going down.

When I told Zail about my diagnosis, once I got out of the hospital, via Facebook, because I was no longer living with him, he did not believe me. Or, more like, he didn't believe it was an impairment or a disability in any way.

"Did you see any gods? Did they say anything to you?"

"Most people need drugs to get into the state you were in. You managed to get into that state all on your own."

Idiot.

Older Hunter had an...interesting...response as well. He thought that the meds the psych nurses gave me in the hospital were what caused my psychosis. Never mind that my psychosis began well before I began getting meds. Read DEAD and you'll understand.

My father also did not believe my diagnosis. He believed that I simply had "emotional problems", that my psychologist was not addressing in therapy. So, she was simply unprofessional. When one of my aunts on my Dad's side visited many years later and saw that my meds were actually being prescribed by real doctors, my Dad never mentioned it again. Before, he had simply said...

"You are not bipolar. Your Mom and Grandma are the ones with the bipolar."

Actually, while I was in the hospital, my mother's side of the family did not initially believe my diagnosis either. They thought that some of the kids at the Retreat had given me drugs, and I was high. They thought i'd be better within a few days. But days turned into weeks...weeks turned into a month...and I was somewhat better but still not stable.

There is another factor at play here. And that is that I was known as one of the most chill and calm members of my family. They thought I couldn't possibly have bipolar, because before Durango my emotions weren't all over the place. I also have an aunt with bipolar, and she is an extremely emotional person. I am not that emotional, as I think you guys already know. And I turned out to be schizoaffective, not bipolar, which fits me a lot better. But yeah. I was so chill and calm that they thought I couldn't possibly be bipolar.

But I was.

I hate it when people make these sorts of statements. At risk of sounding like a Social Justice Warrior, it feels really invalidating. Imagine you've just come home from a war. And then the people around you are saying, "Oh, the war doesn't exist." Doesn't that sound stupid? Well, it sounds just as dumb to say that to someone just out of a psychotic episode.

I think I told you all in DEAD about humanity being out of time. I also told you how I came to this conclusion, or more like how G-d communicated this message to me. However, when I was listening to A BIPOLAR, A SCHIZOPHRENIC, AND A PODCAST, they began talking about akesthesia and how it is a side effect of some psych meds. I was happy, because there was finally a rational explanation for what happened.

However, I missed something important. The podcast said akesthesia is a side effect of anti-depressants. I have never been on an anti-depressant in my life. No hospital has ever given me anti-depressants as far as I know. They have only given me anti-psychotics and mood stabilizers. In my first episode, they may have given me anti-anxiety meds as well (which I do not actually need). Therefore, I am now left without a rational explanation for what happened on 2 NORTH in College Hospital Cerritos. I mean, the rational explanation is that it was all mental illness. But some part of me just cannot accept that. Part of me thinks it was something more. I am not sure I am the Messiah persay, but I do think I have a message for the world. And it's an important message, something the world needs. I am not sure how to get it out there. Help!

We are all twiddling our thumbs while Rome burns. Or, while our planet burns. But come to think of it, sifting through past memories, that wasn't the only part of the message that I was sent to give.

We live in a crazy world. It's no wonder so many of us are in psych wards these days.

We need to be kind to one another. It's easy to pay lip service to this without changing anything in our lives, or expanding our comfort zone. But I think my Aunt Lynn, who runs DBSA Irvine, is a great role model for how to do this. She is absolutely kind and gracious to everyone, except when they try to take over the meeting. Then, (rightfully so), she becomes a bit of a pit bull. I've only seen her like that once. Other than that, she has always been welcoming towards everyone no matter what.

We need to build communities. In a way, I am very lucky to have mental illness. It gives me access to a community right off the bat. That community is DBSA Irvine. I have always felt welcome. I have always felt like I belong. Normies could probably use that too, and not just online.

I also have a general message of love, but that is hard for even me to live up to. It is also hard to express it via the written word. It was easier to convey in the psych ward, in real time. I guess you could say I have a general message of the love of G-d too, without religious boundaries. And as for atheists, well, try to make the world a better place and we'll call it even.

I am the Sybil Ludington/Paul Revere of Messiahs. I can't fight off the British alone, but I can tell you that they are already here. We need to fight back if we're going to have any kind of future worth having. I may be the Messiah, or the Tzadik Hador, but I can't solve all of the world's problems. I can only say that we need to step up our game.

I miss Isaiah. I know it sounds strange to miss a Holocaust Denier if you admire Judaism. But I think of him almost every day. I wonder if he has a roof over his head. I wonder if he has good, healthy food to eat. Most of all, I wonder if he's taking his meds (I met him on the Psych Ward)

What can I say? Of course a girl would miss her best friend. And him and Connie really were my best friends on the psychiatric ward. They were really the only time I had besties on the Ward. And they are the only ones I miss. I miss Connie too. You know what's funny? Once I got out, I called the hospital to talk to Connie. I got her on the line. I told her I wanted to keep in touch. And she, bless her, thought I was actually proposing a romantic relationship.

Now, I wouldn't have said no to that. Connie was pretty cute. And we were on the same page with a lot of things. We would have made a very good couple. But alas, we did not keep in touch. We did not have any sort of relationship, romantic or otherwise.

Isaiah kind of wanted a relationship too. Once, we were about to enter Dayroom when he offered to make out with me. I said no, of course. And I didn't keep in touch with him off the Ward. It could be argued that he would have been a bad influence on me.

I think he would have been.

People had a remarkable way of not paying attention to my depression until it became bipolar. I have no idea why I didn't cut. Maybe I should have. At least people would have paid attention. But that's like saying I should have developed OCD or Borderline Personality Disorder. It's not really possible. You have to be inclined towards it, and I wasn't.

Anyway.

One of the only people who paid attention was Rev. Angela. I only spoke to her once during those years. I knew she was queer, so I was asking her for advice about Jude and what I should do about him. I was very worried about him. But it became very obvious very fast that I was having issues with depression myself.

"Whatever happened to you, it seems to have affected you on a very deep level," she said.

We were standing in the church kitchen, with people swarming around us. Yet we had all the privacy in the world. Because nobody was listening.

I went outside. I think we were all eating cake. We often did that on happy occasions, like baptisms or new member ceremonies. I don't remember what I did after that.

But yeah. She was the only one until Lilith who could tell I was depressed, and more importantly, cared.

I thank her for that. I thank her for offering spiritual counseling, an offer I never took her up on because I guess I was too afraid or didn't know how or something like that. But most of all, thank goodness she had compassion and didn't leave me to die like an animal like everyone else did. I may not have grabbed onto her rope, but it means everything to me that the rope was at least there.

Rev. Angela was the Reverend that I had lunch with on the day of Renne's funeral. We ate Thai food. One of us had some kind of green curry. I was hoping to talk to her privately, but Mom came along. I wanted to tell her my story. Ah well.

At least I wrote a book.

(Reverend Angela is a Unitarian Universalist like me)

I have literally no memories of the times I have been violent while in psychosis. I conclude that the psychosis must have been so severe that I have literally no memory of it. After all, I was on 2 NORTH for six days, and I only remember four. That's a pretty big memory blank. My Mom told me that I have been violent when psychotic. She wasn't there, what would she know, but the nurses probably told her since she was my emergency contact. I've been told I was violent during my first hospitalization as well. In fact, the nurses told me that I yelled a lot of really disturbing shit when I was psychotic.

"You're yelling really disturbing things, Alexandra. There are children trying to sleep here."

Or at least they told me something along those lines. Since my delusions involved children and pedophilia, this just made my insanity feel all the more disturbing.

But yeah. Mom told me that I was punching the air a lot, shadowboxing I guess. I think she meant that I probably mock-punched people a lot too. But I wouldn't know unless I asked. And I don't actually contemplate my psychosis on a regular basis.

I really wouldn't hurt a fly in real life (unless you count eating meat or regularly crossing people's boundaries). Even though I believe wholeheartledly in punching Nazis, i'm not sure I could actually do it. They would all remind me too much of Isaiah, who is the last person in the world that i'd want to punch. Why? Because I think it would be more effective to get him free psych meds, a good meal, and a warm bed. One without me in it, preferably.

I don't think this would work on all Nazis. But I think Isaiah is partially the way he is because of his illness, and I desperately wish I could help him.

You know what the ironic thing is? Ok, so I began to be a mentally ill person really young. Like, fifth grade young. My Mom found out when I approached her, crying, in a St Louis hotel saying that I was worried about being raped. I didn't even know about sex yet. But I knew rape was really, really bad, and I wanted to avoid it. I was terrified. So I was in that hotel room, scared, at maybe...may I guess 5pm?

But later in that trip, we were wandering around St Louis, in not the greatest area, at 3AM, looking for food, and I wasn't afraid at all. Why? My Mama was with me. And I couldn't be raped if my Mama was with me, or so I reasoned.

When Mom and I got back from St Louis (it was a kick-ass trip other than all the anxiety), Mom made an appointment for me to see my trusty psychologist, Kristen. Kristen showed me something called "The Wheel of Worry", which shows how worries can escalate. But just talking to her was enough to make me feel better. I also heard her say to my Mom, "I haven't seen her this anxious in quite some time. We need to keep an eye on her."

The school phobia kicked in less than a year later, at first mildly and then severely. How did it begin? Well, I used to enjoy school. But then my Mom was surfing the NPR (National Public Radio) website, and found School Survival, the website that would lead me to THE TEENAGE LIBERATION HANDBOOK. She didn't bother to vet it before sending it to me.

And the rest is history.

Every once in a while, my nephew threatens suicide. And I always have no idea what to do, because I am not a psychologist. The mental health care in Canada is shit, despite the fact that they have Universal Health Care. The waiting list for psychiatrists is ridiculously long, and the psychiatrist they have assigned my nephew is really, really bad and he can't seem to switch. The psychologist seems to be ok, but i'm not sure if he has one anymore. And I don't think Canada has any peer-led support groups like we do in America. Also, the psych hospitals are really, really, poor quality.

My nephew has developed a healthy mistrust of the medical profession as a result of all this. This is a really bad outcome. Frankly, with all the suicidal ideations he's had since i've met him, it's a miracle he's still alive. But then again, only one of his alters is depressed (he has multiple personalities). The rest seem to be ok. This makes medication complicated at best, because there are young children in the Collective...and the others don't want the children medicated.

My reasoning is that if there is mental illness present, it must affect the entire Collective to some degree. However, Nathan is so compartmentalized that this does not seem to be the case. This makes things complicated.

I have two friends who died young. They are both trans women. One was Renne. The other was named Donna. I have already written about Renne, so I will devote this space to Donna. They were both bi...although in different ways.

I met Donna when I came to DBSA one day. She was really androgynous looking. I looked at her and had no idea if she was a boy or a girl. I was aesthetically attracted to her right off the bat, though. When she introduced herself as Donna, I don't remember how I felt. I may have been slightly disappointed, because I am more into guys than girls. However, I still was sort of interested. When we all got up to leave, I saw a picture of a hot guy on her phone screensaver and figured she was probably straight. *Damn* I thought. But we still exchanged phone numbers. A couple days later, she told me she was autistic and she had a crush on me.

I still had a car, so I picked her up on (Veteran's Day?). I took her to my house, where we sat on the bench in the backyard and discussed relationships, guys, being bi, and all kinds of other things. When she proposed a relationship, I told her I was honored, but wasn't ready for a relationship this soon after Marty yet. I could have kissed her. I should have kissed her. I liked it when she sat close to me.

She saved up her money, bought a big, delicious, expensive dinner, and brought it to group. I absolutely loved it, and thanked her profusely. The next week, I brought her some of my favorite foods. But unfortunately, she wasn't there.

I kept in touch with her after that, though. I still didn't keep in touch with her as much as I should have. And one Sunday, when I was sitting in church, I got a text saying Donna had died.

The night before, I had gotten a text from Donna saying she was suicidal. I did not do nearly enough to help her, I just said "Please don't die on me" because I had no idea what to do. I should have talked to her. I should have gotten help for her. But no. I had no brain.

That Sunday night, I quietly shed a few tears into my pillow. This is my modern-day equivalent of sobbing my guts out. I prayed to G-d that she be safe and happy in the afterlife, if there is one. And suddenly, I felt a bit better. I suddenly knew, without a doubt, that wherever Donna was, she was safe and happy. And at peace.

One day, when I was seventeen, depressed, and walking alone outside at night...in a relatively good mood...I may have saved a life. I was at my Grandma's house, before she lived with us. I lived with her. I often took walks alone at night. Probably not the safest thing to do, but I had less of a sense of danger at the time than I do today.

"I'M GOING TO JUMP!" I heard someone shout.

I stood in place. "DON'T JUMP!" I yelled as loudly as I could.

"Who was that?" the voice asked.

"A ghost," a young, female voice answered.

I clearly was not a ghost, but I can see how she thought that. After all, disembodied voices can often seem like ghosts.

Suddenly, a maternal voice broke in.

"My son has a sick sense of humor. He is going to finish his math homework now. Have a good night," she said.

I did not really see what math homework had to do with anything, but I rolled with it.

"You too," I replied.

I kept going with my walk.

I often have wondered what happened to that boy. I wonder if he just had a sick sense of humor, like his Mom said, or if he was genuinely suicidal. If I came across him today, I would probably try to get him to go to my support group. But maybe "DON'T JUMP!" was the best possible thing I could have told him. You just never know.

Well, at least he'll have an interesting story to tell his children and grandchildren. Or maybe he'll give some speech at some big mental health conference, and i'll be able to raise my hand and say, "That was me!" You've got to admit, that would be pretty awesome.

I believe that everything we do has consequences of some kind, which is why Judaism has so many rules concerning daily living. Those consequences can be good or they can be bad, and I believe that religions with a lot of rules are trying to maximize the good and reduce the bad. These aspects of Orthodox Judaism and Islam make a lot of sense to me for this reason.

But something I don't think these religions address (and I could be wrong, so correct me if I am), is taking responsibility for your actions. I know Judaism has certain teachings regarding forgiveness. Islam probably does too. Christianity considers forgiveness important. I think a lot of faiths do.

Taking responsibility for your own actions is really, really important. It's vital not to say, "I was just following orders," or even, "I was sick." The former is the sort of excuses that most Nazis used when they were finally brought to account for their crimes. And I hear far too many people these days saying, "But we have to!" when discussing filthy things (like the camps) that our government is doing today. To me, this line of thinking is simply unacceptable. Because when we start saying, "I was just following orders," we are on the fast track to Nazidom, which by the way is a complete possibility in today's world.

I hold Nathan's (my adopted nephew's) assailant responsible for his actions, because even if he has a rapist alter...he is still responsible for that alter. And I hold Jill responsible for the threatening actions she took towards me in the psych ward. It doesn't mean I don't forgive her. Of course I do. But I don't give a damn that she was sick when she acted the way she did. The rest of us were sick, and guess what?

The rest of us were peaceful.

I for one do not care if my future husband has mental illness. It's hard enough finding a partner who's accepting of my asexuality/graysexuality. It's hard enough finding a partner, period. I'm not going to sweat it if he has bipolar, schizophrenia, OCD, or anything like that. I would draw the line at Antisocial, and maybe Borderline. However, the Borderline boundary is not a hard and fast one. I have a good friend who is Borderline, and she has a lot in common with me and is a valuable friend in general. If I were into her that way, she might even make a good wife.

I also have a casual acquaintance who is Borderline. Well, she's more than a casual acquaintance. I don't really know what to call her. Her name is Jamie (there! Happy?) and she and I used to hang out very frequently. We never formally dated. However, she carried a torch for me for a long time. I had to break it off eventually because I just didn't feel the same way back. It hurt her very badly, and we had to avoid each other for a long time because neither of us wanted to be around the other. We went on a trip to Mexico together recently, though, and had a pretty good time. So our relationship may be on the mend. However, I have no desire to spend lots and lots of time with her. That's not to say she's not a nice lady. It's just that things between us got a bit complicated.

As I guess often happens with Borderline.

The reason I don't think very young children should be exposed to sexuality is that sexuality is not pure anymore. We as a society have made it this horrible, dirty thing. We have this whole culture surrounding sex that is very sleazy. We have the concept of "sexiness". We just...it's hard to explain. Sexiness is different from beauty. I love beauty. Beauty can be found in a naked figure, or a fully clothed figure. But sexiness is a bit more iffy.

I don't think children should be exposed to this culture. By children, I mean anyone who is below the age of sixteen. I do support sex ed for children below this age, but it really needs to be comprehensive and sex-positive as well as inclusive of asexuality. We also need to teach consent early (and probably first). Otherwise, we need to let kids be kids. The reason I support sex ed for kids, though, is that it may help children undergoing sexual abuse the tools to understand what they are going through and the means to get help. .

Sex in movies is...well...really weird and I didn't feel comfortable watching it as a sixth grader. Mom always told me that sex is a natural, normal part of life. She said i'd understand one day. And I did. I understood when I met Rose. But when we stopped seeing each other regularly, I failed to develop similar feelings for other people.

I wonder...Rose went to the local Waldorf school. Mom wanted me to go there too, but they didn't let me because they couldn't accomedate autistics, or so they said. If I had gone, I would have been around her every day. I would have grown up with her.

Would we be married now?

If I had DID, I know who my alters would be. There would be Natalie, who wears all black and is a writer. She is also Deaf. There would be Courtney, a 27-year-old blonde sociopath who may be a lesbian and who is very fierce in general. Dmitri would be around the same age, always fighting Courtney but less powerful than her. Other than the fact that he has a beard and brown hair, he has no other distinguishing characteristics.

I know these parts of me because during my first episode, these were my voices. Natalie obviously never talked, but the other two never shut up. They never spoke to me, only to each other. They were trying to kill each other at the time too. Natalie was mostly ignored, which was good for her because she was just writing down everything the other two did. That was her role in the SASHA system, which is what everyone called themselves as a collective.

Oh, and I think Natalie was seventeen.

It goes to show, there can be a lot of overlap between mental illnesses. Gabe and Michelle observed this on the show too. They once talked about the fact that they both experienced delusions and paranoia. The only real difference between them was that they both had different labels to describe their illnesses.

Sometimes I wonder what kind of whack it would take for me to develop full blown DID. I certainly came close during my first episode, although I never "switched" personalities. I remained myself the whole time, or as myself as you can remain in a severe psychotic episode. I just heard them as voices, which went away with the right medications.

School phobia is undoubtedly the hardest thing that I have ever had to deal with in my life. I had an aunt who yelled a lot, and a father who was WAY too touchy feely with me. I would take another father gladly than have to go through school phobia again. I would have been happy to go to community college, even though I possibly would have had a harder workload. Mom said no, she didn't believe testing out of high school was possible or "everybody would be doing it". Never mind that quite a few of my homeschooler friends did just that. No, I was forced to choose between Eldorado Emerson and Halstrom, a fucked up choice for someone like me if there ever was one. I had to pick between a loosy-goosy private school or a very school-like homeschool-ish program. I picked Halstrom. But believe me, I would have been fucked either way. Either I would have been forced into an environment where I never could have been happy, and people would constantly wonder what kind of bee was up my bonnet, or I would have been forced to go to a program daily by my Mom, which believe me felt just like school, and I was forced to bottle up my feelings because I knew she'd never understand.

I don't regret my choice. I don't believe I would have been any happier or any better off at Eldorado Emerson. I made the right choice. But it was the lesser of two evils, and by a very narrow margin at that.

The only way Halstrom could have worked was if I only went one day a week, went on an accelerated program so I could graduate faster, and not have Mom insist that I do six hours of homework a day "just like the kids in public schools do". It also would have helped if I would have been allowed to visit my friends in Sonrisa at least once a week without conditions, so I could have kept seeing my love.

But no. That would have made too much sense.

I derived comfort from an odd source after Renne's death. On many days, when Mom and I would drive to the YMCA to work out, we would pass a certain van on the freeway. This van said "Morrow's Plumbing Service" on it. It felt like Renne was reaching out from the heavens, tapping me on the shoulder, and telling me that everything was going to be ok. This van only started appearing on the freeway after her death. I know. I would have noticed if it appeared beforehand.

When I was having some arguments with my Mom about Lilith (she didn't like me dating someone who lived so far off, and in a house that was so hard to find), the van appeared in the parking lot of the YMCA we worked out at. We settled the argument eventually, but the van stopped appearing after that. I don't know why. Maybe it just wasn't needed anymore.

That van, however, was a great source of comfort for me. I have always loved riding in cars, and this was just a plus. I think I may have pointed it out to my Mom once, but I think she was too busy driving to notice. But that's ok. She didn't have the connection to Renne that I did, even though she probably had more sympathy for Renne's family after her death. She cried at the funeral. I didn't. We both cried when we found out she died, her immediately, me later.

So it's possible we both cared, but in different ways. Mom never even met Renne, and I did.

I would give anything for more time with her. I know it would make the blow of her death all the more painful, but that's ok with me. If I could bring her Mama, Ellen, to the shindig then all the better. At least we could all say goodbye.

The only reason I agreed to take psychiatric medication in the first place was because it was obvious to me that my breakdown was due to mental illness and not severe stress.

It was obvious to me because although I was lonely in Durango, I was happy. I didn't have to bother with school. Nobody was making me do homework. So, I didn't do it at all. None of the other kids were doing it either. So I was free from that (major) stressor. I spent my days eating, walking, reading books, attending workshops, and occasionally chatting with friends. I wasn't online all that much either, so it couldn't have been Twitter Psychosis. I only chatted with online friends occasionally. I was too busy living life to be too concerned with them. I honestly did not miss my new girlfriend all that much. Not only was I not really in love with her, I figured I had to look out for myself first. I figured if some kind of escape hatch presented itself, I would take it, and to hell with her and her feelings.

I wasn't the nicest of girlfriends, I admit.

So then an escape hatch presented itself, in the form of Blake's dream mapping workshop. And i started to plan out a life with Renne, with whom I was very much in (platonic) love. And I tried to take it. But then the mental illness took over. Now, Lilith could have been really mad about what I tried to do. She even once said that what I did was sort of mean. But that's as far as her anger went. She didn't understand my depression to its fullest degree. She didn't even try to understand. When I started writing DEAD, and asked her to help edit, she said I should try to find my voice as a writer first before trying to tackle a book. She even said that I should wait for more interesting things to happen to me before I tried writing a memoir. Which is pretty insulting.

Anyway, I don't think I would have been as quick to believe I had mental illness if it hadn't been for that retreat. I think I would have chalked the breakdown up to stress due to school. Mom says I would have met Joel and Lynn, and they would have been able to help me accept my illness. But I don't think my Mom understands just how bad my school phobia really was. I think that would have been the long, hard route to take. I think I would have thought that my family and psychologist were trying to medicate away my feelings, and I think I would have fought back as hard as I could have.

In the book, "My Sister's Keeper" by Jodi Picoult, she says that a true friend isn't capable of feeling sorry for you. But Older Hunter was definitely a true friend of mine. And near the end of our friendship, he told me he felt sorry for me. I think it was a comforting thing to hear. Nobody else around me was telling me they felt sorry for me at the time, so...it was a unique thing to say. And I was sort of falling in love with him at around the end of our friendship. What caused the end? He went away to boarding school and underwent a pretty radical personality shift. He was one of my best friend's Jason's best friend. This was before Renne.

Older Hunter asked if I would visit him in his boarding school (Baylor) sometimes. I said I would. I never kept that promise, and to this day I regret it. I do. He changed. He started swearing. He started sort of getting into sex. He stopped being the sweet boy I remembered and became...something else. I will never send my kid to a boarding school. He became superficial, according to Jason. He eventually stopped responding to my messages on Facebook. I was hurt at the time. Looking back, i'm glad.

I don't consider my friendship with Older Hunter as important as my other friends, because our relationship only lasted for a year. The interesting thing is that he was diagnosed bipolar before I was. He chalked it up to his parents not understanding that he tries to see both the glass half full and half empty in life. And as far as I know, he is not med-compliant. At least, when I told him of my diagnosis, he said, "Are you sure it's not the meds making you that way?"

I already told you guys about my rebuttal to that.

But yeah. I had a crush on Jason. I had a crush on Hunter (at differing times). I had...interesting thoughts...about Nikki. And I often pretended to have a crush on Jude for fun (he knew it was fake).

I may not have been over sexed. But I sure was (in the words of Joel) over SOMETHING.

Now, I would have been perfectly fine without the LGBT Center in my life. However, I question whether I really would have had a life at all. Would I have had the quality friendships I had? Would I have dated? Would I have had an ounce of fun in my life? Yes, nobody in the Center was going through what I was going through. But for once in my life, that was ok. Nobody was asking stupid questions, like why wasn't I in school. That was really important. Even Priya, although she provided an education that I could actually attain, couldn't give me that. So I would say they were both equally important.

Park Day just wasn't the same. I couldn't relate to the other teenagers, who were all into video games and anime. I couldn't even relate to my friends to a degree. All I could talk about was depression. They were all into Les Mis and classic rock. And I preferred world music.

It used to be different. I used to be happy, before Halstrom. It didn't used to bother me that I had different hobbies from my friends. I knew we were the same under the skin. And I had Will (my friend from Priya's/Sonrisa). I didn't used to have to go to Halstrom daily...my life didn't used to feel like a school. So I was a lot happier, and these things bothered me much less.

I am very skeptical of group therapy. I have never found it to be helpful. Admittedly, the only times it was ever tried on me was when I was in a severely psychotic state. During those times, 1 on 1 therapy would probably have been better. I mostly have experience with one on one therapy. And no, peer led support groups are not group therapy.

Group therapy is led by a therapist and controlled by a therapist. Peer led support groups are led by a trained facilitator, who does not try to control the conversation. They simply make sure things are running smoothly.

I think you can tell that I do not really like group therapy very much. This was because, the first time it was tried on me, I only did it because there was nothing else to do and I knew I had to participate in order to get released as quickly as possible. The second time, in Cerritos, the therapist actively ignored me and ignored everything I was saying in order to keep conducting "therapy". I did not find that to be very therapeutic at all. Admittedly, it couldn't be all about me. But did she really have to ignore me?

I benefited more from being in 1 NORTH, where I ran around yelling strange stuff about being the Messiah instead of (by and large) bothering with the group therapy. Well, I did participate quite a bit. But the therapist didn't ignore me. She didn't let me dominate the conversation, but she didn't ignore me either. I am grateful for that.

By and large, though, I benefited more from trying to help others on the Ward (in my own funny, delusional little way), than from the group talks that we had. And I did succeed in my mission. After all, Johanna said I inspired the entire ward. So i'm proud of that.

I encountered anti Semitism twice in the psych ward. One of the anti Semites really scared me, because at the time I wanted to convert to Judaism. The other one, not so much. Their names were Jill and Isaiah.

Jill was your typical bigot who (probably) believed there was such a thing as Jewish privilege, and probably believed that white Jews ran the world. She was scary.

Then there was Isaiah. He was a Holocaut denier. He was pro-Palestine (which many people equate with anti Semitism). Isaiah had also rubbed elbows with white supremacists in the past. He did not scare me in the least.

If you had to make me choose which one I would have to keep within three feet of me for the rest of my life, I would pick Isaiah hands down. Why? He never threatened me. Even though he knew I wanted to convert to Judaism, he still deigned to play soccer with me in the rain. He was willing to discuss his views with me, and to change his mind to a degree. In the end, he decided that Hitler was right to commit the Holocaust...which is scary as hell. But at least he no longer denied that the Holocaust happened. And when he threatened to stalk me, and said I could only stop him by slapping him, he accepted a hard poke on the cheek instead. I know it sounds strange to say that he was actually a sweet person on the inside, but I believe he was. Unfortunately, he was also hateful as all hell towards Jews and probably other demographics as well. So, come to think of it, that cancels any sweetness out.

Oh boy.

So, when I was younger, I once tried to make out with my mother. I wasn't trying to be incestuous. I wasn't trying to be weird. I wasn't even trying to be lesbian. No, I just wanted to know what a kiss felt like. My Mom seemed like the most logical choice of partners for this. I believe this was before I started the OWLS program at my church. I did know about kissing.

Anyway, she really came down hard on me. As she should have. What I did was really, really inappropriate. I question whether she really needed to take such a harsh tone, though. She could simply have said, "We do not do such things with our mothers, Alexandra," and sent me to my room. That's probably how i'd react if my child tried to give me an open mouth kiss on the mouth.

What i'm really grateful for is that my Mom didn't kiss back. Only a really messed up person would do that. But still, if I had grown up in a different household...and done that to my father...who knows what would have happened. And then I could have been blamed, because after all, I would have been the one that initiated things. But I had no sexual intentions at all. I didn't even know what sex was at that age. I knew what romance was, I think, but I don't even remember if that was a factor. I just wanted to know what a kiss felt like.

Creepy, huh? I definitely think so. But this is why I don't agree with a certain class of pedophiles, who say that they will only have sex with a child if the child initiates the sex. The child probably has no idea what they are doing. They are probably confused by the whole thing. It is just as much abuse as when the adult initiates sex. Because a child does not truly understand the implications of their actions when it comes to this.

This is why I still think there should be an age of consent. Admittedly, we need to make looser rules for teenagers. But age gaps should be more regulated than they are. What happened between Kyle and my nephew should be illegal. I don't know how much older Kyle was, but my nephew was only twelve and that should always be considered wrong. Twelve is way too young to be doing anything with anyone. And a three year age gap should be unacceptable. Adults forget what a big difference three years is at that age. Two years is a big enough deal, even at seventeen. When I was a seventeen year old in love with a nineteen year old, she seemed really "big" and really old to me. Now I consider a nineteen year old a pipsqueak.

I think that when you are a teenager, you should only date within a year of your age. Either a year older or a year younger. Anything more is just asking for trouble. And if they want to "play around" with age, they can do that as adults.

"Kill them all."

"No. Accept them."

Thus went our conversation about trans women in the psych ward.

We repeated this exchange a few times, with the other guy laughing in astonishment. We then began discussing atheists.

"I have no problem with atheists. I was raised by atheists."

"But you see, that's part of the problem."

Looking back, I have no idea what he was talking about. But I think I probably understood then.

"I don't know if you're God or the Devil."

I crossed my fingers.

"They're close, huh?"

"Yeah," I said.

    And it's true. People often say that we can be a good influence or a bad influence in other people's lives. But people never mention that we can be both.

    And people never mention, in conversations about morality, that evil often masquerades as good. And thus, it can be extremely hard to tell the two apart. In Renne's words, "foul foul people don't wear nice name tags". Or something like that.

    But back to what I think of atheists. I still have no problem with atheists. In fact, I have a little deal to make with you guys. Just do your best to make the world a better place and we'll call it even. I don't know if there's a heaven or not, and I can't really speak for G-d, but I personally do not have any beef with you guys. So that may say something. After all, I was raised by atheists.

And trans women are just women. There is no need to be threatened by them. There is no need to drown them. There is no need to set them on fire. Would you do that to a cis woman? No? Then don't do it to a trans woman. End of story.

I am bad at keeping track of dates. When Lilith told me our anniversary was important to her, I damn well enough kept track of that. But I have forgotten since our break up. And as such, I have forgotten the exact date that I began to experience symptoms of schizoaffective for the first time. So, I have shifted the date to the nearest holiday.

I consider Thanksgiving my anniversary. This is fitting, because when my illness hit...I was thankful for my illness. It had hit a couple of days before, and I even formally gave thanks for it at Durango's Thanksgiving Dinner. I obviously didn't (entirely) know I was very ill though, not until later. I thought I was enlightened. So I gave thanks for my "enlightenment". It was a welcome relief after years of pain. And Renne gave me hope, after years of being at the mercy of my family.

The holidays are stressful, but I love this time of year. I am generally responsible for cooking the turkey these days, since I am so good at it. Christmas was my favorite holiday as a kid, but I think now it may be Thanksgiving because of all the food. I also have fond memories of cuddling with Zoe after Thanksgiving dinner, although things got weird between us pretty fast.

Ok, so I am mostly asexual. I realize this conflicts with one symptom of bipolar/schizoaffective, which is hypersexuality. I am not hypersexual in my daily life. I am not even typically hypersexual during episodes. However, I am more sexual than I otherwise would be. If I didn't have mental illness, some of my sexuality would go away.

Hypersexuality is a symptom of bipolar disorder. Since I have schizoaffective, and that is a cross between bipolar and schizophrenia, I experience this too (to a degree). Sometimes I have thoughts of being a sex worker. This is by far the most embarrassing symptom I experience, because I absolutely hate the sex industry. These thoughts do not happen often. They do not generally happen when I am well. In fact, I hate the commercialization of sex in general. I realize legalization of it may be necessary to preserve the safety of the women within it, but I still hate its guts with all my being.

If I were a sex worker, I would be a sort of "rent a friend" type. I would also do my work wearing cat ears. I would not have sex with any of my clientele. I would act more catlike than I usually do. I might let people stroke my hair. I might sit on laps. I might cuddle. I would definitely talk. In this way, I would be a lot like a therapist, albeit a therapist cleverly disguised as a sex worker. And i'd get my doctorate too. I know this is confusing, and does not sound like sex work. But this is the sort of thing my brain dreams up. Mentally ill brains do not often make sense, especially when they intersect with asexuality.

If I were a stripper? I'd dress modestly, for a stripper. I'd wear a sports bra and a miniskirt. And I definitely would not take those off. I may wear other clothes over them, but I would strip down to them and that's as far as i'd go. I'd make a serious study of dance, and not just pole, but ballet and bellydance as well. Also, i'd read aloud excerpts of my books at every dance. They'd remember me. I'd be known as the Literary Stripper.

But yeah. This is probably my most embarrassing symptom. On paper now, it doesn't seem so bad. But it's still humiliating, like the sex industry has found it's way into my head.

You realize this has very little to do with sexuality and far more to do with symptoms of mental illness, right?

      I am not repressed. I don't secretly want to become a prostitute. I am not secretly allosexual and hiding it. This is just what my psychologist calls a "thought disturbance". It's not a sexual fantasy. It's a thought that sometimes comes into my head that is so bizarre that I could totally buy aliens from Area 51 planting it into my brain. This isn't about sex at all. This is about mental illness.

One time, I was house sitting for Joel and Lynn. They were away, having adventures with Lynn's brother Ace in Senegal. In fact, they were away for a month. I was effectively under house arrest, because I was afraid to use Lynn's car. Mom took me to school, although my friend Joseph did take me to my final exam. Mom also took me to therapy. But other than that, I was basically home alone. And this got really difficult really fast. I started crying a lot. I welcomed this. I felt like I was finally feeling the pain of the past, when I had been numb to it for so long. I was still with Marty. I'm not sure if we were talking, though. Maybe we were in another one of our fights. I don't remember either way.

Anyway, I emailed a whole bunch of people. One of the few people who responded was my old Zen master, and my old gender therapist. My gender therapist gave me a hotline to call. My old Zen master had some questions for me, which I answered. We had a short email exchange, and it comforted me to know someone cared because Glenn obviously didn't (I had emailed him, with no response. I write about him in DEAD ON THE VERGE OF BLOOMING).

Mom was not initially very supportive. She said, at first, that nobody wanted to hear me complain and that they all had jobs and better things to do. In my anger, I kicked her out of the house. I had to do this a few times before she'd listen. She left for about half an hour. She then came back, apologized, and said she never wanted to be like that again. She moved in with me for the rest of the stay.

My friend Karen said that led to my second psychotic episode.

I have been in the interesting position of visiting the psych ward as a visitor, while I was still very manic. In this case, my Mom and I were visiting our friend Reece. He was high as a kite. He was talking fast. He definitely looked like he belonged in there, too. I remember him begging my Mom for a chess set. He said, "There's a Target right next to this hospital. It doesn't have to be expensive. Just leave right now, and get me a cheap one."

"But the social worker won't be back until morning," Mom said.

"That doesn't matter. Just go get it right now. Drop it off tonight."

Mom, I thought *get him the goddamn chess set. It's true the social worker won't get here until the morning, but she can give it to him first thing in the morning or disapprove it. Reece won't have to waste a whole extra day without a chess set.*

"I don't understand," Mom said.

"Just get the goddamn chess set," Reece said.

I think visiting hours ended at that moment. That, or Reece lunged at my Mom. I don't remember what happened.

When I was back at the hospital, I desperately wanted a copy of JUDAISM FOR DUMMIES. I looked forward to visiting hours every day, partially because of visitors, and partially because each day was the day I hoped Mom would finally get a copy. I tried to make it as clear as possible that I wanted JUDAISM FOR DUMMIES. However, once I got out of the hospital, my Mom presented me with a copy of CHICKEN SOUP FOR THE JEWISH SOUL. "Here," she said. "Here is a copy of the book you've been begging for."

I think I laughed. "No! I wanted a copy of JUDAISM FOR DUMMIES! But thank you anyway!"

Mom took me to the Barnes and Nobles in Fashion Island to get me a copy. But the closest thing they had was IDIOT'S GUIDE TO JUDAISM. Not what I had hoped for. Oh well. The reason I had wanted a copy of JUDAISM FOR DUMMIES on the psych ward was because I wanted to learn more about Jewish law, so that I could update it for the 21st century. I know the FOR DUMMIES book series was a poor place to start, but Asim offered to teach me the Torah...so I wouldn't have been so bad off if I had decided to go that route. However, I didn't. I started going to Temple instead, and eventually stopped when I realized I just couldn't take their views on Israel and intersectional feminism.

I wonder why people are split up into different units the way they are. I wonder what the difference between 2 NORTH and 1 NORTH is, other than the superior quality of care for the latter. 1 SOUTH seemed to have more men and drug addicts in there, yet there was Connie and an older lady there as well. I don't think it was the violent ward. Nobody in there seemed particularly dangerous to me, although Brandon was rather annoying. Come to think of it, Maria was there as well. So it probably wasn't a men's ward. It may have been for petty criminals, as well as anyone who just couldn't take 1 NORTH. There was at least one brain injury patient in there.

This is a case where the ward that seems most like the Hilton isn't necessarily the best ward. 1 NORTH was ok, they had more perks, but they really should have had better control of Jill. They should have stopped her from terrorizing the other patients the way she did. That sort of thing never would have been tolerated in 1 SOUTH. The others probably would have punched her in the face, especially since most of the patients on that ward were men.

Come to think of it, that may have been another reason why I felt comfortable there. When I was feeling at my most unsafe on 1 NORTH, I ran into one of the men's rooms for safety. What I was trying to say was that I literally would have felt safer sleeping with a bunch of men around me than in my own "safe" girls' room. I have almost always preferred having male friends most of the time. And this may have been another reason why I felt safe on 1 SOUTH, despite the fact that the anti Semitism may actually have been worse. I mean, at least he wasn't directly threatening me.

Sad.

When I was walking through 2 NORTH to visit Reece (who was on 1 NORTH), the patients happened to be out. One spotted me. His name was Joseph. We immediately recognized each other. He gave me a hug. I was glad to receive this hug. I hugged him back.

"Did Victoria file her complaint?" I asked.

"Yes! And so did Johanna!" he replied.

"Good!" I said.

"Keep on wearing that hat!" Joseph then told me. "It'll earn you a place in Jamba Juice!"

I was wearing a dark red scarf, in a messy turban. I don't think it was my best scarf day. But I was still flattered. One of the other staff moved us along. So I couldn't talk to him further. But I was very happy knowing he was watching over my fellow patients, and that they were being taken care of in this way.

And by the way, i'm not put out that he said my scarf would earn me a place in Jamba Juice. I know he meant that it would earn me a place in heaven.

And I am honored by what he said, even though I know there's a lot more to being a good person than just dressing modestly. Wendy Shallit, in A RETURN TO MODESTY, makes a case that dressing modestly is an integral part of being a good person. I have read her arguments quite a few times, and to me they make zero sense. You can be a good person in a bikini. You can be a terrible person in a burquini. You can be somewhere in the middle in board shorts. You can be somewhere in the middle in a hijab.

People tell me i'm a good person at least once a week. To me this is total bullshit. I've done bad things in my life. I've said hurtful things to people I love. I've also done good things. I've also done bad things while meaning to do good things. So there you have it. I don't think i'm horrible, but I don't think i'm the good person everyone says I am either.

So i'm not sure I believe in toxic people. I mean, I certainly believe in Zoe. She was toxic. She was also a sociopath. But other than that? I'm not so sure. I once heard the truism that "we're all the bad person in someone's story" or something like that. Or, "we're all the villian in someone's tale". Oh dear, I hope that made sense.

One thing listening to A BIPOLAR, A SCHIZOPHRENIC, AND A PODCAST has taught me is that we are all capable of being both villians and heroes in someone's story. Hell, we all are villians and heroes all balled up into a person. Nobody is all good or all bad. Sure, some people are more good and some people are more bad. But nobody is entirely one or the other.

I have unfortunately met quite a few people who are on the sociopath spectrum. Luckily, these interactions were online...so I wasn't in any real danger. One was named Donnie. The other was named Kenny. I already have written about Zoe quite a bit in the other stories, so I won't cover her here. So you know how the marker for a sociopath is that they can't feel love or guilt, right? And they are usually good at reading others? Well, Donnie pretty much fit all of those criteria. Except that he did love one person.

Hey, it's a SPECTRUM.

He really loved his ex-girlfriend, Mara. And not in the sense of being a stalker. He genuinely, truly loved her. Said she was the only person he only ever felt close to. And that says something right there.

Kenny used me as a sort of moral compass, because he asked me what I thought of a really fetish-y anime and then used that to express his opinion on his own Wall. When he told me he'd never loved anyone in his life, I blocked him.

Sayonara, socios.

Dennis made the remarks he made out of ignorance to my actual situation. Not only that, he genuinely didn't want to understand. He believed he was right, that I was a sheltered little girl that was "fashionably gay", and that I needed to be thrown into the deep end. He thought he was right, and that I was wrong for wanting to avoid school at all costs (you can't hang around LGBTQ teens and be completely innocent for very long).

Lilith, on the other hand, wanted to understand me. I just didn't have the words to explain it. She could tell I was depressed, and wanted to know why. I couldn't tell her why. It was frustrating. But she was the original "service animal". She followed me around, tracked my moods, and asked me if I was ok if I didn't seem ok. No one had ever treated me that way before. It was one of the reasons why Lilith pressuring me into dating her wasn't completely horrible for me.

"Service animals" are what I call people who can read others so well that it's scary. As soon as you have a thought that is slightly out of the ordinary, they can tell. If you are bored during class, they can tell. If you are feeling depressed at Models of Pride, they can tell. It's a very creepy talent these people have. And no, these are not normal neurotypicals. Lilith was autistic like me. These are people who are really good at reading people.

I've come across three of these people in my lifetime. Lilith, Claire, and Anna.

You know about Lilith. When I was in massage school, Claire and Anna were two of my classmates. Anna was somewhat sadistic towards me. She enjoyed giving me massages that were so painful I screamed. Claire simply talked to me. I couldn't relate to her worldview, but I did my best to interact with her.

Let's just say I strove to be focused in class.

I think that when people say, "Control your emotions" or "Control your mind", it's the dumbest thing i've ever heard. I can't control my emotions. I can't control my mind. That's one thing having a mental illness has taught me. It's taught me that I have no real control of either. I don't know how anyone possibly could. It would be like trying to hold back the ocean, or trying to channel the wind. We can control our reactions to our emotions or our thoughts. We can also control the way they appear to others. But we can't control our actual emotions or our actual thoughts.

I don't know why people act like we can. It seems to me like the cruelest gambit in the history of the world. Like someone decided someday to pretend that we have control over something we in reality have no control over. That reminds me of this thing in America, that people genuinely believe that people born into desperate poverty can become millionaires. And we call it the American Dream. This name is very apt if you think about it, because it really is only just a dream. In no other country do we have this delusion. America deserves to be locked in a giant psych ward for believing this. I can't give you stats, there are people who can make a much more intelligent argument on this than I can. But really. Really.

Then there are the idiots who believe we can cure cancer with more veggies, crystals, or special bottled water. Honestly, this is just cruel. Or the people that think we can cure mental illness with special meditations. Or, with the above. Which really is just cruel. We already don't want to be sick. And the people that peddle these are just giving us false hope, that we can be normal people. I mean, we totally can be. I am in many ways. There is hope for people with mental illness. But it lies in medication, therapy, and peer-led support groups, not in crystals, asparagus, and special bottled water. If crystals could cure mental illness, we would be using them on a mass scale already. No, this is one instance where conventional medicine is the way to go.

Sorry, holistic healers.

I would like everyone here to know that i'm happy. Ok, i'm not giddy. I'm not manic. But I am happy. I am content with my lot in life. I live a life that I am reasonably proud of, and I am doing the things that give my life meaning. You really can't ask for anything more.

Well, content may be the better word for what i'm feeling. You may ask how this is possible for a person with mental illness. Aren't we supposed to be unhappy all of the time? And if not unhappy, too happy? No. I have news for you, bitches. I'm mentally ill, and i'm happy. I'm not really sure how I got here, but there you have it. I take a good combo of meds, I go to regular therapy, and I go to support groups led by my adopted Aunt Lynn. I am on break from school right now, but I am using this break to work on this book that you are now reading. I'm majoring in Psychology, which is the field I truly love. I found this field because I took a career test and Psychology was my second result. Artist was first. I am glad I decided on Psychology. Artists are so boring (Matthew excepted). Mormons are more interesting to me.

ANYWAY. I'm not normal by any stretch of the mind, but I may be more normal than I thought I was. Remember the beginning, when I said that I am schizoaffective, a cat therian, and non-binary? I'm starting to question those things. Again.

The main reason I thought I was schizoaffective was because I always thought my emotions were flat. But how can I compare that to others? I can't get inside someone else's head. So there's really no way to know how flat I am relative to others. My psychologist thinks i'm schizoaffective though, because I have thought disturbances (like my version of sex work) in addition to mood swings. So maybe I will leave the diagnosing to her.

As for being a cat therian, it's true that I had "cat ears" as kid, ears I could really feel. But I retracted them, and I haven't been able to get them back. Since I can't get them back, maybe i'm not a therian anymore. But maybe I should talk to someone wise about these things.

As for being non-binary, I have successfully lost a whole load of laundry in the shuffle. Losing a sock or two is one thing, but this is ridiculous! As a result, my closet has become much more feminine, and I would feel ridiculous being openly non-binary while dressing this way. Note that I am not entirely unhappy with this change. I am more annoyed than anything else.

Mom and I used to be very active in border activism. One of the things we did was that we actually visited Tijuana. Now, Tijuana has a bit of a reputation in the American mind. It is known for drugs and crime and drinking and general debauchery. However, it is actually one of my favorite cities in the world. Tijuana is pretty safe as long as you know what areas to avoid, which everyone on that trip did. So we visited sites where deportees from America were being cared for, and listened to tales about the stigma against them (people tend to think they're criminals). But by the far the saddest stories I ever heard were the tales of deported veterans. That's right, there are couragous young men and women who serve our country in Iraq or Afghanistan, put their lives at risk, and then they are deported once they finish their term. If that isn't disgusting, I don't know what is.

These veterans often have PTSD like any other veteran would.

So one day we visited the border wall itself. We observed how it stretched into the sea, for quite a distance. I hadn't taken my lithium that morning. I began to (sort of) cry. I was thinking about how Jessica would probably be deported soon, and how uncertain her entire situation was. I was thinking how it would be possible to swim around the wall, but that anyone who tried would probably get shot. Mostly, I wanted the goddamn wall down. A certain veteran had printed a poem on it, and had signed it Amos. There was an American flag on the wall too, plus a series of names.

I think they were the names of Veterans, but I am not sure.

Incidentally, I can't sleep in situations where other people can. For example, if I haven't taken my meds, I can't sleep at all. If I take my meds, it takes forever to fall asleep. However, it does happen eventually. I also cannot fall asleep in a sitting position. I was once on a plane with Jamie on a red eye to Canada where I was trying really hard to sleep but just couldn't. I fooled her. She thought I was fast asleep the whole time.

The exception is that once I was on a Buddhist meditation retreat, forgot to take my meds that night, and was fine. But that was before my second episode. I don't think I could pull that off today. Even if I could, I would have to spend about six hours a day meditating. Goodbye to living a normal life. And I probably would still have symptoms to boot, because there is more to mental illness than just severe insomnia. So yeah. Not worth it.

I value sleep very highly, as you can probably see. I like to sleep. I don't like to get up early. I can, but I don't like to because I can't just go to bed early and fall asleep early. I also pretty much cannot nap. I can in really exceptional circumstances, but by and large I can't. So I try really, really, hard not to have to get up early. I schedule all my classes for afternoon classes. When I worked, I worked afternoon shifts. I don't know how I managed being assistant dishwasher at De Benneville Pines, and working all those morning shifts. Maybe I was hungry for breakfast.

Another thing I value highly is sex. I know this sounds really weird for a graysexual, but it's true. If I ever have sex again, I am adamant that it will be with someone I genuinely love and care for, as well as regularly have sexual thoughts about (which seems to be my version of sexual attraction).

Oh well.

I do not feel like I am in recovery from mental illness, nor do I think I ever will be. I don't really want to be, either. For one thing, I still think I have the potential to be the Messiah so that would knock me out of the unofficial definition. For another, I think the whole concept of recovery is stupid.

We stole the concept of recovery from the addiction community, which is a huge mistake. Mental illness is not a drug. We are not addicted to our illnesses. Conflating them in this way is really dangerous, because it invites the same sort of stigma that the addiction community faces.

I consider myself (mostly) in remission from mental illness. You can't recover from mental illness. Mental illness is a chronic illness. It is permanent. You can't get rid of it. Ever. Last time I went manic, my Mom thought I had recovered from my mental illness. This is why the concept of recovery is dangerous. Because it promotes the thought that we can "magically get better" when we can't and we'll never be anything but ourselves.

To a degree, this is a stupid argument. We have bigger fish to fry than worrying about simple words. Gabe is right about this. But words do matter. Not that I would ever bother someone on their choice of words. Really, it's none of my business.

However, Gabe is right that there are more important issues than words. It's kinda like Human Rights Campaign and Gay Marriage. To a degree, gay marriage is really important. But now that we have it, we seem willing to forget about homeless LGBTQ youth, hate crimes against trans women, the fact that in several states it is legal to fire someone for being gay, and so on. We think that now that everyone can get married, the fight is over. It's not. It's really not.

The reason we fought so hard for gay marriage was so, during the AIDS crisis, people could be at the sides of their lovers when they were dying of AIDS. The AIDS crisis may be over, but we seem to be forgetting about everyone else.

Chaiya's coat is red, with broken buttons and a secret pocket. It keeps a soul warm in cold weather. It is plaid on the inside. I got it on the Psych Ward, where a woman named Chaiya gave it to me along with some Judaism. I gave her my leather jacket in exchange. It was not a fair trade. That jacket never kept me warm.

"That's a really nice leather jacket," Chaiya observed when we were making our little exchange. I looked at my Mom.

"May I?" I asked.

She nodded.

I took off my leather jacket and we exchanged jackets. My Mom says I broke the buttons when I banged the jacket against the door of my room in anger or fear, I don't know which.

Chaiya reached inside my jacket. No, this is not girl-on-girl porn, she was simply showing me the secret pocket on the inside. It had a hood, so I could be Little Red Riding Hood. The leather jacket didn't have a hood though.

The zipper on Chaiya's coat is broken now, but I still keep it. I will always wear it with pride.

I wonder what happened to Chaiya. I do think about her quite a bit. I know she lived in Whittier, but other than that I have no idea where or how to find her. I wish I hadn't lost her number when she gave it to me. I'm not a lesbian, i'm pretty sure i'm not even bi, but I was still sort of interested in her. In what capacity, i'm not quite sure. But we could have explored that together. I'm not too hung up these days on gay/lesbian identity anyway. If I had fallen in love with her romantically, that would have been great. If I had formed a sort of platonic partnership with her, that also would have been positively supreme.

However, I also would have not wanted her to get hurt. People do things in mania that they woudn't otherwise do. Flirting with Chaiya may have been one of those things.

You know how Gabe occasionally complains about Michelle vaping on A BIPOLAR, A SCHIZOPHRENIC, AND A PODCAST? Well, I have a complaint of my own to make. And it's about my nephew, Nathan.

Nathan has DID, so not all of his alters do this. But a couple of them vape, and it drives me up a wall! I want Nathan to have a good, long life, and i'm afraid he won't if a couple of his silly alters insist on indulging this stupid habit of vaping. Nathan is really, really smart so he knows what arguments to use on me when I bring this up. But I still know i'm right. And I really do worry about his health. My Grandma's partner Ron died of lung cancer, and i'm interested in helping Nathan avoid the same fate.

Some alters vape. Others prefer cigarettes. Others, I imagine, don't smoke at all. But even part time is worse than no time. I'm obviously glad Nathan doesn't vape full time. I am glad not all of the alters vape. But still. I'm worried. I know Michelle does it to relieve stress. I wonder if Nathan does the same thing. G-d only knows the poor kid has enough stress in his life, what with the PTSD and all.

To a degree, I need to mind my own beeswax. It's not my life. It's his. But since I am his Aunt, it does concern me somewhat. I just don't want to be a nag. I've already made enough mistakes. For example, I put his deadname on a package to him (I was afraid it wouldn't get through customs if I used his preferred, non legal name), and he couldn't touch the package all day. I felt so sorry when I found out.

Mom would make a great drug dealer.

Once, when we were in Texas and I was hypo-manic, she gave me some of her seizure medication. This actually isn't as dumb of a move as it would seem. There's a lot of overlap between bipolar and epilepsy, which is what my Mom had at the time. When a bipolar person is manic, similar structures in the brain fire to when a person with epilepsy is having a seizure. I think. Don't quote me on this one.

But anyway, Mom gave me some of her seizure medications and it worked. I was still manic, but I didn't spiral upward into psychosis. My psychiatrist at the time, Thuy, gave her shit about this because Lamictal should never be given all once. You are always supposed to titrate up, or some of your skin can turn black and fall off. This actually can be a life threatening condition, so Thuy was right to ball my Mom out. But Mom was also right to give me the drug, because it worked so well at containing my mania.

She eventually stopped giving me her medicine. I think we went up on my Risperdal as well. But that was the vacation where I started seriously writing DEAD ON THE VERGE OF BLOOMING. That was the first summer after Renne died, the first summer after the episode. I told my step aunt I wanted to write, and she got me a pen and paper. I wrote a poem. Then I started writing down all the quotes I could remember, from everyone. I didn't trust the people around me with my feelings very much. So I trusted the notebook. I had an Ipod with Afghani music at the time, and I blasted that into my ears while scribbling quotes into the notebook in the backseat of the car. It was a fun, fun time.

Fine vacation, indeed.

So I am responsible for the fact that one of my cats only has half a tail. Why? I was talking to Mom in the doorway of the garage once. I shut the door. The cat was around my feet. I thought he would move out of the way. He didn't. I slammed the door on his tail. He screamed. *Oh shit* I thought. We immediately took him to the vet. He wouldn't stop meowing the whole way there. The vet shaved the injury. Part of his tailbone was showing. I winced inwardly. "G-d, if I had an injury where part of my spine was showing...I'd be screaming too," I said. The vet said we'd have to amputate part of the tail, because there wasn't enough blood flow for the tail to have a full recovery.

So it was amputated part of the way. I felt horrible for the rest of the day. Or, I thought horrible. We were given antibiotics and pain meds to give to him. I apparently gave enough antibiotics, but way too much pain meds. Since it was a controlled substance, we couldn't get a refill. The nurse even insinuated that we just wanted it for ourselves, so we could get high. Mom and I were both furious. So he didn't have any pain meds for the rest of his recovery, since I accidentally gave him too much the first few days.

And I am royally pissed. I am pissed that an animal had to suffer because of our stupid laws. You think our laws do anything? If a drug addict really wants drugs, they'll get them, laws or no. What these laws do is make life more difficult for the people who really need them. I mean, look at what Michelle has to do with some of her meds. She can't get certain pills a single damn day early. Jesus Christ. And an innocent cat has to suffer because we're worried about a grown woman and her grown daughter getting high.

Jesus.

Another thing that pisses me off about my former cuddle buddy, Mark:

He once said he thought someone's delusion was "creative". Excuse me, fucker, this is a psych ward not a fucking art institute. Would you say that to someone with cancer? How fucking creative is prostate cancer? Is puking from chemo a unique expression of their soul? No? Well, then there is no reason you should appreciate someone's mental illness for it's unique aesthetic qualities either. Maybe we should put people with pneumonia in art museums, if we want to take this train of thought even further. We can forget hospitals. There's something so beautiful about the sight of them slowly dying, something melodious about their slow coughing. I mean, seriously. What are you even thinking?

This line of thought implies you have a level of control over your delusions that people just don't have. It's called mental illness for a reason. I wasn't a prisoner of conscience on 2 NORTH. That woman wasn't a talented actress acting as Cleopatra. She had a real mental illness. A mental illness that you laughed at. That you found funny. You found it amusing when Chaiya said that you, Tink, Mom, and me all had Jewish souls. You weren't honored and flattered, like I was. You treated her like a joke. You treated me like a joke. And I will never accept that.

It's not empathy. Bipolar/schizoaffective is not "cute". You are no different from those asylums in the Victorian era, where people would pay to enter and laugh at the patients. You did the exact same thing for free, because you were my "friend", and it is disgusting.

I suffer from something called Imposter Syndrome. In my case, that means that when you declare an identity, you are afraid you are not really that and you're just being a drama queen or something.

Take therianthropy. A lot of people probably would think therians are insane if they knew more about them. I mean, a human that identifies partially as an animal? Transgender people are bad enough.

Non-binary? You dress exactly like a normal woman, kid. You're just trying to be a special snowflake.

Bipolar? You're just being trendy, never mind the circumstances from which you got it.

Schizoaffective? What the hell is that? Are you sure you didn't buck your diagnosis for something more shiny? Are you sure you should have this much say in your own diagnosis, anyway? Why should you ask questions? Shouldn't you mostly leave this to the doctors to decide? Emotional flatness? Well, how can you really know that for sure? You don't seem flat to me. Thought disturbances? Well, how bad are they really?

Tzadik Hador? Honey, you're probably just the craziest bitch who ever lived. Plus, you're not even Jewish.

It all goes back to…

Bisexual? You're just lying because you want to belong. You shouldn't have taken the microphone. Other people have things to say that are more important than yours. You are too young to know whether or not you're bisexual, anyway. You have to have sex to know for sure.

(Never mind the existence of biromantic asexual identities.)

(And yes, I did have the bisexual part said to me in real life. In the back of a dark car. In an angry voice. It was hell on earth.)

It is really stupid that we teach kids to follow their dreams in this culture. Because of this, they are wrecked when they find out that following their dreams isn't always possible. That may be one of the reasons the depression rate in our country is so high. We set our kids up for failure. We say, "Shoot for the moon. Even if you miss, you land among the stars."

We shouldn't be shooting for the goddamn moon. We will never get to the goddamn moon. However, the stars may be a bit more doable. Every famous person in this culture got this way by following their dreams. So they tell their fans to follow their dreams too. But for every famous person who made it, there are thousands of people who didn't make it. Nobody ever goes to them for advice. I would advise anyone going into the arts to find a day job that they love. Don't settle for flipping burgers unless you can absolutely avoid it. My minister acts on the side. But yeah, never study your art in college. Use that to get a degree you can use to get a decent day job. You don't want to be working at Goodwill (if you're disabled) or Nordstroms (if you're not disabled) for the rest of your life. Trust me. You will hate your job, you will hate your life, and you will be too tired at the end of every day to pay attention to your art. So get a decent day job. Get a day job that you truly love. That's why i'm getting a Psychology degree instead of an English degree. Because although Psychology isn't writing, I do like Psychology a lot. I'm lucky to have this passion as well.

I was wrecked when my dreams of unschooling failed. But it wasn't just the loss of a dream that had me down. It was realizing that I wasn't going to be allowed to live according to my conscience because I was under eighteen. I really did see schools as morally wrong, as strange as that sounds. So being forced to succumb to that system day after day...killed me.

The main thing that A BIPOLAR, A SCHIZOPHRENIC, AND A PODCAST taught me is that there can be a hero and a villain in the same person. It told me that no one is entirely bad or entirely good. As far as I already knew that, I really needed to hear it again. Gabe used to be an absolute monster. He used to yell at his wife and cheat on her with everything that moved. Since starting treatment, he has gained some merit. But he is still that person, to a degree. And he is still this person.

There are so many people I could write about here. But i'll write about my mother.

Mom used to be my torturer. She used to lay down the law, and enforce it with no regard for my well being whatsoever. When I tried to tell her I was having problems, she didn't listen and in general just didn't understand. She dominated my life.

Fast forward to November 2011. She visits me in the hospital daily. She brings gifts. As soon as the others tell her to transfer me, she transfers me to UCLA (probably the best hospital in Southern California). She continues to visit me. Mom turns into a gentle, caring person. When Renne dies, Mom starts crying immediately, unlike me, who has more of a delayed reaction. Mom drives me to both funerals, no questions asked. She even drives well above the speed limit so we can get to the first funeral on time. Although we've had our arguments ever since, by and large she has become a better mother.

One of the things that makes it hard to get care is that not all psychiatrists are proper psychiatrists. I am talking about Progeny Psychiatric here. When I went psychotic for the second time, we called and called and my "psychiatrist" could not be reached. Mom later found out he wasn't actually a psychiatrist. I don't know what he was doing administering psychiatric medication. Maybe he was a student. But that was when my Mom decided I was done with finding my own psychiatrist, and she would find them for me instead.

So I was once visiting this "psychiatrist" (I have no idea of his name), and I innocently asked him how he was doing. He said, "Oh, I just broke up with my girlfriend," and gave me this really weird look. I am glad I was wearing a long skirt and a head covering. They felt like armor that protected me from his strange glance. We proceeded with the appointment, with no additional weirdness. Blanche would have been proud.

No hanky panky.

But really. Our lives as mentally ill people are hard enough without giving us fake psychiatrists to work with. Fake psychiatrists that cannot even be reached in case of an emergency are not useful psychiatrists to have. Like, at all. The psychiatrist that I have now responds to all of my emails and calls pretty quickly. Like, within the hour. That is how your psychiatrist should be, too. Anything less is unacceptable.

This argument has been going on since the dawn of time.

Mentally ill people vs their parents and families.

Now, I personally think both have their place. As long as they stay within their respective spheres, everything is fine. There are some things that a parent, no matter how kind and devoted, will never understand about what it is like to be mentally ill. And there are some things that a mentally ill person, no matter how empathatic, will never understand about what it is like to care for or otherwise parent a child with mental illness.

The problems begin when the two groups try to invade each other's space. There are some things that a parent has no right to say or give advice on. Those matters should be left to a peer. There are things no mentally ill person has a right to say about their caretaker. Those caretakers should go to other caretakers (and maybe a psychologist) for support.

I would like to stress that it is never ok for a parent or other caretaker to act as though they know what it's like to have mental illness. They don't. And they never will. Not even if they have a mild version, like my friend Jamie's (Asperger's Syndrome) or Aunt Lynn's (cyclothymia). That's actually one thing I really like about Aunt Lynn. She stays within her sphere. The mild version can help with empathizing with a person with mental illness. But it's not the same thing at all.

Another thing I like about Aunt Lynn is that she actually says what she means, and takes her beliefs as far as they should be taken. Most people say they believe in "Love Your Neighbor, No Exceptions". Then they turn around and attack pedophiles, who frankly, as much as we hate them, are also our neighbors. I distinguish between pedophiles and child rapists, who I frankly do hate.

At one point, I thought that I might be a pedophile. And I was able to discuss that within Lynn's support group. Nobody judged me. Do you know how rare that is? Granted, I was fairly nervous. And if I actually were a pedophile, I might have come under scrutiny. However, people in her support group were kind to me. More importantly, Lynn herself was kind to me. I have never felt judged by Lynn, ever.

Lynn has always been a good Aunt to me. Sometimes we disagree, and she makes her opinion known. But that's rare. Lynn and I agree on most things. In a way, I have taken Lynn as my mentor and role model the way my "friend" Neil thought I should. I just don't slavishly copy her every move. I consider her a role model for not judging people, and being kind.

Romance with autism spectrum disorders can be an extremely obsessive thing. Squishes and squashes can be very obsessive as well. Granted, even in neurotypical circumstances, all of those things can be obsessive. But with autism, it is bumped up to one hundred. Breakups are the same way sometimes. We're not trying to bore you. It's just literally all that's playing on our mental track, and it takes something very compelling indeed to turn that boat around. This is harder to do when you have autism. Usually an obsession will fizzle out on it's own. An obsession is seldom lifelong, unless it's a passion for sailing or something like that. A passion for sailing can last a lifetime. I should know, because I don't sail.

A passion for writing can also last a lifetime. But that doesn't mean i'm thinking about my next writing project every single moment of the day, like an obsession. More like I get obsessed for a short burst of time, complete a project, and move on.

I'm not sure if a passion for a person can last a lifetime. I have known my Mom my entire life, but i'm not sure you could say that I have a passion for my mother. I don't think i've met anyone who fills the spot of a passion in my life. A passion is like a cool, chill, form of an obsession. It's like a cycle. You keep coming back to it, no matter how far you stray temporarily. This tendency can be disastrous in love. You can't leave a person and come back to them after a while, and keep doing this, and have a good relationship. The other person is alone part of the time. They'll cheat. Or you could have a polyamorous relationship, where that person could have a constant partner and you'd be going in and out of their lives.

I once heard that sometimes boys do this to each other in their social interactions. They'll be friends with someone for a while, leave for a while, then re-engage the person and resume the friendship where they left off. I think these are called "rust friends". Ignacio may qualify as a rust friend for me, if we manage to continue our friendship where we left off when he, a Mormon missionary, was transferred to Buena Park and stopped proselytizing at my school. And I really do consider him my friend. He may have been trying to convert me to Mormonism, but he has all my books but GALATEA...so I consider him pretty high in my ranks. I just wonder how much he will have changed when I see him next. I also wonder how much I will have changed.

It is hard to explain the difference between criticism and meanness. Sometimes it is a very fine line.

Ignacio would probably say that all same-sex relationships are doomed to fail from the start. The thing is, I have no snappy comeback. Sure, Marty lasted two years. I would call him a success. He technically was a same-sex relationship. But can you really call someone who was born intersex and was fed female hormones against his will a same-sex relationship? What about Zoe? She barely counts, because she was a pathological liar and I only dated her for a month. However, she had a weird mix of hormones in her body. She was about half and half, slightly more female than male. Then there's Lilith. You could make an argument that this was a heterosexual relationship, since Lilith was biologically male when I dated her. However, I could not honestly call this relationship a happy one. It wasn't miserable, but it got pretty damn bad at the end. Ignacio would probably count it as a same-sex relationship because it got so bad. You see what I have to live with here? How confusing all of this is?

Ignacio would probably wonder at the poor, confused Unitarian contrasted with the seemingly solid, happy Mormons. And I cannot stand this for the life of me. I don't like being held to an impossible standard. And i've seen very few happy relationships around me, period, Michelle and Cherie excepted.

Sometimes my Mom thinks I am exaggerating when I discuss certain things with her. It bothers me, because i'm not. Ignacio and I were talking about LGBTQ rights once, and he mentioned that in his home country (Chile), they kind of brush people off when they come out as trans. Like, they accept it, but they don't take it too seriously. This bothers me too. I don't believe that people should be treated like that, at any age.

Dennis was happy to have an overdramatic teenage daughter. He was happy to brush off my suffering. It meant I was filling the appropriate social role for my age. And Dennis was happy to oblige me. It was really sick, honestly. If I had attempted suicide, he probably would have brushed it off as a "cry for attention", the way he did with everything else I did.

My Grandmother believed something even more stupid for a while. She used to believe (I sincerely hope she doesn't believe this anymore), that suicide is the worst form of revenge. She thought it was a form of hostility. Before I left for Durango, my Aunt attempted suicide. We all visited. We all were as kind as we could be. I never would have guessed that after Durango, the tables would be turned.

Let me tell you what suicide really is. It's wanting the pain to stop. And it's not knowing any other way to stop the pain. Suicidal people don't want to die. They want to live. They want to live without the pain. I wanted the pain to stop. I had no power to stop the things that were causing my pain. I don't know how I held on. I was completely powerless. I just reached the end of my rope, at like, fourteen, and held on for dear life for three years while everyone around me thought everything was fine. I never saw anything like it. People really are stupid. Not to mention, every time I tried to get the pain to stop, I was rebuffed. So I just had to live in pain. I was left to die like a fucking animal. I was left to suffer.

Mental illness is often called invisible. But it's not. It's only invisible when people are too stupid to listen to you.

In one sense, i'm very lucky to be mostly asexual. I never have to worry about what a sexual partner may or may not think of my body. So I can be a bit more confident than I otherwise would be. I can go after the most good-looking guy in the room, and have complete confidence in myself.

I now realize that I am rather fat, and most guys wouldn't be interested in me in that way. By and large, this isn't really a problem for me. However, now I sort of know how Lilith may have felt. "Why would such a nice-looking girl want to sleep with me?" she may have thought. I was IDing as demisexual at the time, so she may have chalked it up to our emotional bond. Which was both strong and not very strong at the same time. I did used to be rather good-looking before my second hospitalization, where I gained like fifty pounds.

The thing is, I don't look any different to myself than before. Jamie occasionally complains about how i'm all fat now, but I see no difference between my past self and my present self. To me, I always looked about two hundred pounds. So to me, there's literally no difference. When I look at photos of my past self, i'm mildly shocked and I wonder how I could possibly have thought I was fat. But whatever.

Food in mental hospitals is generally not very healthy. It is mainly meat and carbs, very little (if any) vegetables and fruits. This may be part of the reason why I gained so much weight, even though part of the time I was on a kosher diet (where the portions were very small)

I don't miss growing up without a father figure in the home. I think it was a great exercise in growing up with less of an influence of the patriarchy than usual. Mom didn't even allow Disney movies, which can present some pretty twisted ideas to a girl. I went to AstroCamp. I was part of a "book club" called Space University and totally loved it. I was encouraged to excel in the arts more than math and science, but other than that I had a fairly feminist upbringing. And i'd like to provide this for my child as well.

As much as I am attracted to men, i'm not sure I want a father figure in my child's life. I don't need a father bugging my child about staying thin (which is what my Mom did to me as an adolescent), calling my daughter "girl", saying she should get into modeling if she's thin, asking her to eat less appetizers when they're around, saying he has no love or respect for her if she deviates from the norm, treats her like garbage if she has feelings, and other shit like that.

Most men mean well in this day and age. And most men would probably make good fathers. I still don't want to take the risk. However, i'm still attracted to men and I still want a male partner. Maybe i'll do what Mom did, and have a partner but not allow him a major role in my child's upbringing. And i'd keep a close eye on him, and how he treats my child. At the first sign of trouble, he can scoot.

What got me through the rest of high school was:

1. Medications
2. A relaxed school environment
3. Writing

     In that order. Without medications, I would have been too insane to participate in society in any capacity. In a regular school environment, I would have just broke, even with the medications. And without writing, I would have had no way to heal from what I was going through. Renne's death really brought me to my knees. Writing gave me the means to express my pain, not just from Renne's death but from my broken dreams as well. I really needed that. I needed a way to finally make myself understood, and spread awareness about THE TEENAGE LIBERATION HANDBOOK and what a game-changer it is.

     Although these things differ in importance, they were all needed in order to live an OK life. I couldn't have coped without any one of those three. I think Dennis thought I was a lot stronger than I really was. He thought I was strong enough to cope with a regular public school environment. I wasn't. I needed a relaxed pace, with relatively simple work. Plus, public school would have triggered me to the nines. I didn't need that when I had just been diagnosed with bipolar with psychotic features. That's a best case scenario, too. In my state, I probably would have dealt with all kinds of bullies as well. I did not need that in my life. That probably would have been the straw that broke the camel's back...again. Breaking twice would have been just cruel. And teens can be like vultures. I've heard that they have a way of preying on the weak.

     I was not bullied significantly at Halstrom. Kids thought I was strange, but I cultivated that image to keep them the hell away from me. I would not have made friends in public school. I would have been way too sad. And ultimately, I would have went down. I know that for sure.

And Dennis would have no clue why. He would mock me for not being strong.

I love Weejie (aka Nathan) more than anyone else outside my biological family. Ok, so i'm not quite sure what love is, as a feeling. I'm sure i've felt it. I'm not a sociopath. I can feel happy in the presence of certain people. I can look forward to seeing certain people. When certain people leave me, my world is significantly altered. I think about certain people a lot. I send some people gifts joyfully. I guess, to me, that's as far as it goes.

Love is sort of a hard word for Nathan. He associates it with all kinds of abuse. For him, the word love is connected with abuse. He is trying to change this. But the fact that he never tells me, "I love you", is fine with me. It's enough that he considers me family.

I hope that someday I can buy a Class B RV, pick up Nathan, and travel all around America with him. He doesn't know that I have this particular dream yet. But I also do not want to rip him away from everything he knows and loves, unless he is completely OK with that. I also am not sure that i'm ready for driving a large van. I would have to become a chaplain first, because in that situation i'd want to become a travelling preacher and preach at different UU churches across America.

Still, Nathan is an exercise in letting go. The more good things happen to him, the less he needs me. I want good things for him because I love him, therefore I have to learn to let go. I will never have the relationship with him that I want because I don't live close to him. And he's probably not interested in moving in with me and being with me forever, the way I wish we could. I'm not even his closest family relationship. That would be his brother. And that's probably as it should be.

I understand Moms with Munchausen. Because if I truly did not care about Nathan's well-being, I would find subtle ways to hurt him to get him close to me again. That's what Moms with Munschausen do. That's the real why of Munchausen. It's an inability to let go and let their kids grow up and leave them and form other important relationships in their lives the way kids always do. And then the Mom is left behind. Forever. Or maybe the relationship just changes. It grows more distant, sure. But hopefully someday that kid will come back and take care of you. And then you will be consoled. I know others will think i'm wrong on this, but I do think i'm at least partially right.

I am definitely not a perfect person. One of the lines in old version of HEYA = HEYA could easily be interpreted as anti Semitic. I can be caustic. I can be arrogant (which seems to be a Unitarian Universalist thing). I don't run around deliberately trying to hurt people. That is good, because I seem to hurt people by accident a lot. Just look at Marty.

Even worse, people tend to minimize or excuse the damage that I do. It's because I give off this aura of happy innocence. In some ways, i'm very true to this impression. But it doesn't stop the fact that I often hurt people by mistake. People make excuses for me all the time. It's disgusting. It's a major disadvantage of being as…(charismatic?) as I am. When people think you're this wonderful person, they think you can't seriously hurt people or cause major emotional damage to people. And in both cases, they're deeply wrong. This has hampered my personal growth a lot. For instance, I wish my behavior towards Jude had been stopped in it's tracks. We might still be on good terms today if it had been. Of course, Jude didn't visit me when I was sick…but that was more his Mom's fault than his. His Mom was the one who didn't want Jude to see me in the hospital. That's why Jude was never told where I was, or when visiting hours were. I'm sorry to speak ill of the dead, but it's true.

"We have enough problems of our own already," the most un-Christian words that were ever said.

My "friend" Neil thinks I am a failure. That is fine with me. He is one of those people that knows how to run everyone's life but his own. For instance, he thought I should go into computers as a career when I have no interest whatsoever in computers. He is not supportive of me covering at all, either. He kept posting My Stealthy Freedom pictures on my Wall. I love My Stealthy Freedom, but that doesn't mean I want to show my hair. He even sent me a picture of a semi-nude woman once, which was totally inappropriate. Neil was even dumb enough to think that asexuality and lesbianism are the same thing, and that my covering met all of the requirements of Islamic Hijab. That's even what he called it, hijab. And he calls me the failure.

I just have no words. I shake my head, over and over. I remember he once said he wished he could pull my scarf off my head. I of course take great offense to this.

I remember before I started covering. This was after Seema, but before Wrapunzel. I was at the LGBTQ Center. Laura was giving away a bunch of clothes, including a light scarf. I was wearing workout pants, and a shirt that covered my collarbones and upper arms. I took the scarf, and draped it in a sort of loose hijab style that wasn't quite hijab but came close.

It felt so damned right.

I wore it for the rest of the session. Someone said I should wear it more, if it felt that right to me. So I walked home in it. "HOLA MARIA!" someone shouted at me from a car. I smiled. It was the only time i've ever liked being catcalled. I took it down when I got home, but when I discovered Wrapunzel eventually, I knew it was what I wanted to do. I haven't worn hijab style since (I prefer the Jewish tichel style), but it just felt so good.

I also used to own a big blue square scarf. When I prayed to Renne, I would use it to cover my head. This was before I knew about some Christian women covering their heads in prayer. But it felt right in that instance too. I wrecked the scarf trying to turn it into a veil, but oh well.

I cover partially in Renne's memory. Renne was a young woman who meant...I don't remember how I felt about her. I don't think I was in love. But there was this connection between us. It was stronger than romance, because I got a girlfriend short after I met her and I tried to leave my girlfriend to be with Renne. However, I came down with mental illness and she died shortly thereafter. She was nineteen years old, which seemed like so old back then and so young now. I remember how I would cover my head when I would pray to her spirit, and occasionally when i'd do witchcraft. I also do it to acknowledge my connection to Renne's spirit, sort of like how Orthodox Jewish women cover to acknowledge their connection to their husbands. I realize the concept of me being married to Renne's spirit is problematic, since she can't consent from the grave. However, it is basically that idea. Renne continues to play a huge role in my life, even though she's dead. If money were no object, I would spend all my time travelling and selling DEAD ON THE VERGE OF BLOOMING, as well as my other books. I would happily devote my life to her memory. I may yet do that, if I find a way to do so and still make enough money to care for myself.

I also cover my hair out of modesty. I don't cover all of my body, because I simply can't. It's not practical for me (autism). I try to cover my legs, as best I can. I wear t-shirts because I value artistic expression in my clothing, and can't get that with the state of long sleeve clothing as it is. I do not show my chest, or I do my best to try to avoid that. Why modesty? It reminds me that I am more than my body. Now, Contemporary Psychology says mind and body are one. But for me, it is comforting to transcend the body in this way. I don't know why this is. Perhaps it is because I don't feel very attractive, or I don't feel completely comfortable in my body. But that doesn't bother me very much. I don't feel a big need to change these realities. To me, they don't matter.

I do not believe my covering results in more respect for me. I once went out in a miniskirt, thigh-high socks, a tank top (my breasts were bound down), and was treated with the greatest respect by strangers. I went to school in a babushka style wrap, a long skirt, and long sleeves, and was horribly cat-called to the degree that I did not feel safe taking my usual route to school for the rest of the walk. I don't really care about this. However, I hate it when modest women say they get more respect from people when they cover. This simply has not been true for me. It also contributes to a lot of slut shaming, and subtly implies that immodest women don't deserve the same respect that modest women do. Men never worry about this kind of crap.

I'd say my chest is medium. Lianna once commented that I don't have a small chest. Since she's a therapist, she's probably right. However, I don't have a huge chest either. It has never really had a lot to do with my life. I have a binder in my closet to make it look more masculine if I want that, but I very seldom do these days. People don't really notice my chest much, I don't think. I have never really considered what I want people to notice about me physically. I try to express myself through clothing, but i'm not trying to accentuate physical traits. I guess that is the heart of modesty.

I do feel better about my appearance when I cover. I used to feel really weird about my hair. My hair never really felt like "me", so I feel better when I cover it, even though it's pretty and looks nice. I mean, I never really minded my hair. I never really felt dysphoric about it. But it never really felt right, either. Covering it with a scarf helps manage these feelings. I'm not sure why my hair doesn't quite feel like me. I only really knew I felt that way when I got that haircut at fourteen, that got all masculine by accident, and then finally felt like me. But I never have gotten that feeling back. I have shaved my head. It was fun for a few days, but then I went back to covering. I just like how covering looks better. And i've dyed my hair twice (blonde-pink), which was awesome, but I still like covering better. I can't hide emotions while covering, because my coverings do not cover my face. However, I do have two face coverings at home. I like them. My Mom doesn't. She draws the line there. I like them because they accentuate my smile.

My coverings are simply my coverings. They are additional items of clothing that I choose to wear. I like them to be pretty. I like them to add to my overall beauty. And that's just how I feel.

Mental illness is a life-threatening illness. We make it more of a killer when we add police who don't understand mental illness to the mix. Remember that homeless man who was beaten to death in Fullerton? I was appalled. People can't control when they're sick. And when they're sick, they typically can't control their behavior or follow orders. Acting like they should be able to is ableist as fuck. I've caught therapists in psych wards spouting this nonsense. I told one that if we were always able to control our behavior and how we reacted to things, none of us would be there.

Depression is a killer through suicide. Bipolar and schizoaffective have the depression element, but they also have the element of either psychosis or extremely reckless behavior. Both can lead to death. At the very least, when they go untreated, a person cannot achieve their fullest potential in life. That is a death in itself.

Apparently police do not understand mental illness, although this may be starting to change. There are police at Meeting of the Minds every year. They typically give a seminar on drug use in teens (what else would you expect from cops). But I think (or at least hope) that cops are there to learn as well. Otherwise, they may as well stop wasting everyone's time (although drug addiction is a very real issue).

However, I understand why police are scared of mentally ill people that are aggressive. When my bipolar aunt is angry, she is absolutely terrifying. It doesn't matter whether or not she has a weapon. When she is not angry, she is a relatively peace-loving, pleasant person to be around. She is a good listener. She is typically nice. But she is absolutely (and I hope she won't take issue with this) terrifying when she is angry. She has this yelling voice that makes you want to go to the corner of the room, curl up into a ball, and die. Not all yelling voices have that quality. Not even all mentally ill people's yelling voices have that quality. But hers does.

I can only talk from my perspective, so I can't confirm the following for sure. But I think people are taught to fear mental illness. This is to everyone's detriment.

When I was doing my second intake at Cerritos, my intake officer left the room for a moment.

"That was some pretty good acting you did there," said Mom.

"Look, I have never lied about my feelings and I don't intend to start now," I replied.

"Everyone acts about their feelings to some degree. It's how we express ourselves."

Huh?

I don't remember how I replied. But I remember thinking she was absolutely bananas, and must not have any feelings at all if she felt the need to put on a constant show for people.

We have not discussed this little exchange since my hospitalization. But it was sort of insulting. It was as if she thought my mental illness was just some act. Now, I know that's not true. Mom has seen me straight up insane. She has seen me absolutely nuts in both my first hospitalization and my second. But I still wonder exactly what she meant by that.

I wasn't even that emotional. I just teared up a little.

"Schizophrenics don't usually tear up," the intake officer said.

I thought I might be schizophrenic at the time. Where I got that notion, i'm not sure. But I have been rediagnosed as schizoaffective since, by a professional, so I apparently was half right. It was just me, my mother, and the intake officer. Thank G-d they let me in. Do you know that you can only get into a hospital these days if you are a danger to self or others, or if you are at risk of becoming gravely disabled? That's like saying you can only go to the hospital for heart disease if you have a heart attack! Granted, we have psychiatrists. But sometimes delusional people don't fit those criteria, but still need the hospital.

There was a time when I was seeing a GP (General Practitioner, in other words a regular doctor), for my psych meds. I don't think doctors are technically supposed to do this. But mine did. Mine prescribed lithium and Risperdal for me for quite some time. It was good. We saved money. Mom was confident I would never go manic again, and that I was on the right medications. So she figured I didn't really need a psychiatrist.

One problem.

I went manic.

Granted, this did not happen when I was seeing my GP. This happened when I was seeing my "psychiatrist". So nobody had any idea what to do. It was like being swept out from shore, waving for help...with no lifeguard there. At first Mom thought i'd recovered from bipolar disorder. I'm not sure when she realized something was wrong.

When things can go this wrong with a "psychiatrist", imagine the fireworks that can go off with a General Practitioner. My point is that mentally ill people really should be handled by psychiatrists. It says something about our mental health care system that not everyone who needs one can afford one. And a lot of mentally ill people can't hold down a job, me included. That's not some moral referendum. It doesn't mean we're lazy. It means we can't hold down a job for long periods of time. That's not to say I won't be able to someday. I just can't right now, plus i'm a student. So that places extra financial constraints on me. I think though, that everyone deserves quality mental health care. Financial status shouldn't matter here. Anyone who thinks it should is a judgmental prick.

That reminds me of an argument about education that I once had with Marty. He said, "Yes, wealthier people deserve a better education!" That scared the shit out of me. Education is the great equalizer in our country. It is the means by which the poor are supposed to be able to get a leg up. That can't happen if the rich are getting it better than the rest of us. Granted, I was homeschooled. The quality of homeschooling can be affected by money. It doesn't have to be, though. Here, in Orange County, it is possible to take community college courses for free. We also used to have Park Days, where kids could meet friends for free. Ditto for writing club and classics book club. A lot of those things no longer exist. Admittedly, I wouldn't put my kids in public school. But that's because schools aren't democratic, not for any other reason.

There are advantages to having autism. I am not going to steal anyone's intellectual property here, so if you want to know more I suggest you Google it. There was a particularly good article I read on the subject, but I can't seem to find it just now. However, it stated that one advantage to having autism is that you can have very close bonds to certain animals.

This is definitely true. Marty had a very close bond with his cat Jack before he died. His bond to Jack was probably greater than his bond to me, and I have no complaints about that. When I was younger, and more autistic, I also had a very close bond with my bipolar Aunt's dogs. Their names were Duke and Prince. One was a beagle, the other was a dachshund. I helped train Prince, who was quite stubborn. I took them on walks and played with them. When i'd sleep with my aunt at night, the dogs would often sleep with us. My aunt was very close to them as well. She didn't have a job, she was way too disabled to work. So she spent a lot of time caring for her dogs. She adored them. So did I.

My memories of the dogs are actually pretty hazy. This is not due to trauma. It's just that my memories of my childhood are pretty hazy.

I was diagnosed with bipolar at age seventeen, and began taking medications at that age. I once heard that I had been diagnosed with major depression earlier, and had been recommended for medication but had never received it because my Mom thought I was too young to need it. But this has never really been confirmed. Still, I think my anxiety about being raped as a fifth grader...I think it all started there. That was my proverbial snake in my Garden of Eden. Of course, this would assume temptation and an element of choice. Neither were present there. It was all suffering.

It may have been a good thing that I was not medicated at a young age. For one thing, there's no guarantee that I would have accepted the medications. For another, using adult psych meds on a teen can lead to suicidal thoughts and/or actions. I could be dead now. Also, I could have thought that they were trying to "medicate away my feelings". I don't know what this could have led to, but i'm sure it wouldn't have led anywhere good. Maybe my Mom would have forced the meds down my throat. Either way, i'm sure things would have been much crueller than they eventually turned out.

I do believe things turned out for the best, except for Renne's death. I wouldn't have done anything differently. I think it was right that I went to Durango. I don't regret that at all. I don't really regret falling through the cracks. I don't think anything my psychologist could have done would have helped much anyway.

When Mark decided he didn't like my head coverings, it was partially because it made me "different". But I have never had a problem with being different. I have always been different. I was different because of the autism. I wasn't just different because I had a label slapped onto me. Autism really does make people different. We're not just ordinary children with a label. If we were, there'd be no need for the label.

We don't like to play with other kids. We often like to read. We often prefer animals to people. Etcetera. All of those things set us apart. Children notice these things, and bully us. Now, I mostly escaped bullies. But that doesn't mean there wasn't some fairly vicious backtalk about me. I didn't care at all, bless me. I still enjoyed going to school. I still had a decent life. And I was able to eventually move on to environments where this didn't matter.

Mental illness makes you different too, but less so. You just have to take meds daily, and see special doctors. Sometimes you have to explain long absences, due to psych hospitalizations. You sometimes have to explain irrational behavior. True friends stick by you. Fake friends don't. It's a great way to winnow out assholes.

Still, I think autism makes you more different than mental illness does. Autism is more innate, mental illness less so.

Why do people think it's so bad to be different, anyway?

MY THEOLOGY

1. Humanity has run out of time.

2. God is in pain, because of how we are treating the planet and one another.

3. There is no afterlife/ Live like there is no afterlife

4. Doing good is more important than believing in God.

5. Humanity can choose good or evil. God either is choosing to let us do evil, or cannot stop us from doing evil.

6. LGBT people deserve equality and should be accepted.

7. God does not control everything. God cannot control humanity's actions.

ACKNOWLEDGMENTS

Thank you Matthew Nishii, Gabe Howard, Michelle Hammer, and Mama!

Made in the USA
Columbia, SC
11 March 2020